THE MIND
AT WORK

THE MIND AT WORK

HOW TO MAKE IT
WORK BETTER FOR YOU

J
153
LUCA
c.1

BY EILEEN LUCAS

*Diagrams by
Sharon Lane Holm*

*The Millbrook Press
Brookfield, Connecticut*

Photographs courtesy of New York Public Library Picture
Collection: p. 16; Monkmeyer Press Photo Service: pp. 24
(Merrim), 30 (Conklin), 34 (Anderson), 36 (Forsyth), 68
(Forsyth), 81 (Strickler), 94 (Forsyth); Bettmann Archive:
pp. 57, 76 (both), 89.

Library of Congress Cataloging-in-Publication Data
Lucas, Eileen.
The mind at work : how to make it work better for you / by Eileen
Lucas.
p.   cm.
Includes bibliographical references and index.
Summary: Explains current knowledge about the human brain and
how it works and suggests ways of improving such skills as creative
thinking, memory, and problem solving.
ISBN 1-56294-300-6 (lib. bdg.)
1. Thought and thinking—Juvenile literature. [1. Thought and
thinking. 2. Brain.] I. Title.
BF441.L74 1993
153—dc20   92-34663 CIP AC

Published by The Millbrook Press
2 Old New Milford Road
Brookfield, Connecticut 06804

Dedicated with heartfelt thanks to
William Shirer, my high school history teacher,
and Jeanie Luckey, my high school librarian
(now a history teacher), two individuals
who challenged me to use my mind and
encouraged me to believe in myself.

CONTENTS

THE MIND
AT WORK

INTRODUCTION

How would you like to be a genius? Maybe you'd settle for success in life, whatever that means to you.

You can have it, you know. You can live up to the standards set by Leonardo da Vinci, Albert Einstein, and other great persons.

But in order to do that, you need to take control of your thinking and learning processes. You need to understand and take care of your brain and the body that houses it. This book will try to help you with that. Think of it as a sort of owner's manual for your mind. In it you'll find information on how the human mind works, and how to make yours work better for you.

When you get a new toy, game, or any sort of electronic equipment, you usually get a set of directions with it. And if you want it to work right, you'll learn as much as you can about it.

Your mind should really be treated the same way—it's the most fantastic piece of equipment you'll ever use. But as you've grown up, you probably haven't been given very much information about it. Instead you've been taught various "subjects," like reading and math and geography, and somehow it was hoped that you would figure out how to use your mind along the way.

The mind is much too important to take for granted. The following chapters will give you a glimpse at some of the ways the mind works.

THE WORK OF THE MIND • There is a word for the work that the mind does. It is called cognition. Cognition is a process that includes perception, learning, remembering, and all the things we call thinking.

Cognitive science is the study of the mind at work. It looks at how the brain grows and how the ability to learn and think develops throughout our lives. It identifies the milestones that are reached and passed along the way. By looking at some of the processes of cognition, perhaps you can learn to use your own mind better.

• Perception is the input stage of cognition. It is the way we receive information. It involves the senses—sight, hearing, touch, and sometimes smell and taste. (For example, a small child sees a four-legged furry creature.)

• Learning is the encoding or filing of input. (The child's mom tells her the four-legged furry creature is a dog.)

• Memory is the storage and retrieval of information learned. (The child sees the same four-legged furry creature again. She remembers that it is a dog.)

• Thinking is information processing—the way information learned and remembered is manipulated. (The child sees another four-legged furry creature. She compares it to what she remembers about the other. This one is bigger and a different color. But it makes the same noise. She asks her mom, "Dog?")

In this book we will try to look at each of these activities separately. But in reality they are often all going on at the same time.

SEEING THE COGNITIVE PROCESSES • The cognitive processes are invisible. We cannot see thoughts, even when the skull is open during surgery. But there are ways we can learn about thoughts. One way is by introspection; that is, inspecting our own thoughts and thought processes, or thinking about thinking. You may find yourself performing some introspection while you are reading this book.

Another way is by using technology to measure activity in the brain. Electroencephalograms (EEGs), magnetic resonance imaging (MRI), positron-emission tomography (PET), and computerized axial tomography (CAT) scans are examples of sophisticated brain imaging techniques that are now available to doctors and scientists. They give us pictures of what is happening in the brain, which is very helpful in figuring out the mysteries of thought and behavior.

A third way is by watching behavior, which is the result of thinking, and then using a person's behavior to figure out what he or she may have been thinking.

There are limits to all of these methods. But they are all useful in giving us glimpses of the mind at work.

THE MEANING-MAKING MACHINERY

The workings of the human mind have long mystified people. Even though people have been around for several hundred thousand years, we really didn't know much about what makes us tick until relatively recently. There is still much that we don't know. But when you consider that the Greek philosopher Aristotle believed the heart controlled our feelings and thoughts, and that as late as the seventeenth century there was still debate among philosophers as to the roles of heart and brain, we've come a long way.

PLACES IN THE BRAIN • Today we know that it is in the brain that thinking takes place. Developments in neurochemistry (the chemistry of the nervous system, which includes the brain) have led to increased understanding of learning and thinking. Much of what we do (perhaps nearly all) is regulated by chemical reactions in the brain.

Structurally, the brain stem handles the automatic responses (such as breathing and heart rate) that keep you alive. It is located on top of the spinal cord, through which messages are communicated between the brain and the rest of the body.

The cerebellum is a slightly more advanced section of the brain. It coordinates messages between your brain and the

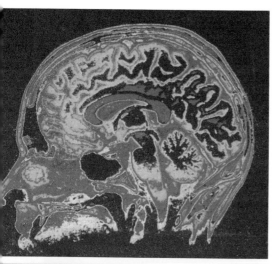

A magnetic resonance image (MRI) reveals details of the structure of the brain.

A positron-emission tomography (PET) scan shows the level of activity in different parts of the brain.

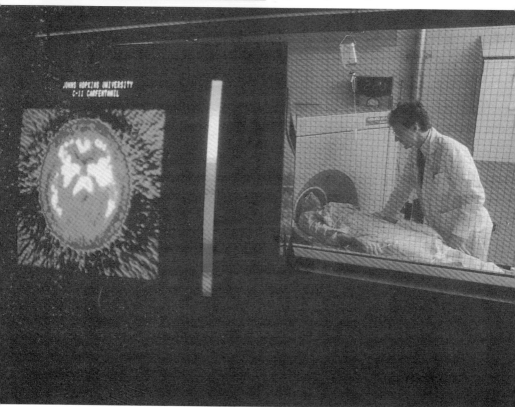

muscles in your arms and legs. Some of the memories that allow you to perform numerous physical activities without having to consciously think about them (like walking, throwing a ball, riding a bike) are stored here.

The limbic system is the next most developed part of the brain. It is a group of structures in the center of your brain that play an important role in regulating the way you feel. One of these structures is a grape-sized gland called the hypothalamus. The hypothalamus deals with many of our primitive emotional responses, such as eating, sleeping, fighting, and mating. Another is the hippocampus, curved in shape like a sea horse or a ram's horn. This structure is connected to sensory input systems and plays a vital role in memory. The thalamus is a nearby region about the size of a walnut. It is involved in the reception of physical sensations, such as pain and heat or cold.

At the top of the brain is the cerebrum, the most recently developed part of the brain. (It is only about 200 million years old, while the brain stem first appeared in animals about 500 million years ago.) With the rest of the brain working to keep you alive, the cerebrum is free to do advanced thinking. It is with the cerebrum that you learn and think and dream. The cerebrum is the part of the brain where all the things that make us human happen. In relation to the rest of the body, this area is much larger and more developed in humans than in any other animal. This is why humans have much more capacity to think than any other creature.

THE CEREBRAL CORTEX • The cerebrum is divided into two halves, called left and right hemispheres. These hemispheres are connected by a thick band of nerve fibers called the corpus callosum. The entire cerebrum is covered by the cerebral cortex, a layer of nerve cells $1/8$ inch (3 millimeters) thick. The cerebral cortex is where advanced brain functions occur. The cortex is divided into four lobes: parietal, occipital, temporal, and frontal. Each lobe has a number of important jobs to do.

The parietal lobe seems to assemble information from various places in the body. The occipital lobe receives messages

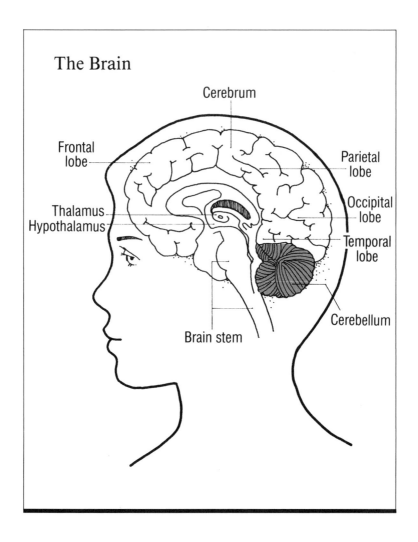

The Brain

Cerebrum

Frontal lobe

Parietal lobe

Occipital lobe

Thalamus
Hypothalamus

Temporal lobe

Cerebellum

Brain stem

from the eyes and controls our vision. The temporal lobe has several functions. One portion of it is dedicated to our sense of hearing. It also plays a role in language and memory. The frontal lobe has a number of management functions. It is involved in directing much of the work of other parts of the brain.

The left and right hemispheres look much the same, but they function in very different ways. The right hemisphere controls the left side of the body, and the left hemisphere controls the right side. Thus, when you move your right hand, the signals are coming from the left side of your brain.

In most people (about 90 percent) the left hemisphere is dominant, or stronger, than the right side, and most left-dominant people are right-handed. People who are right-dominant are mostly left-handed. But some left-dominant people are left-handed, some right-dominant people are right-handed, and some people are able to use both hands equally well! (Or they use one hand for some activities, like writing or eating, and the other hand for other activities, like painting or batting.) These people are called ambidextrous. Some people are better at using both sides of their brain than others. These people might be called mentally ambidextrous!

There are some dramatic differences in the ways that the left and right hemispheres operate. We will look at these more closely in Chapter Five.

NEURONS AT WORK • Every thought you have, whatever part of the brain it comes from, results from a complicated sequence of electrochemical events that take place in the brain. These events are interactions between nerve cells called neurons. Neurons are one of several kinds of cells in the brain. They are sending and receiving messages all the time, even when you're asleep.

Each neuron can receive information, in the form of nerve impulses, from thousands of other neurons and can send information on to as many as a thousand more. Scientists estimate that there are about 100 billion individual neurons in the human brain, so you can see that the potential for connections is virtually limitless.

Information enters a neuron through its dendrites, armlike extensions that receive impulses. That information then travels down to the cell body. The cell body produces a new impulse, which is carried down an extension called the axon. The axon branches into many terminals. The place where an axon terminal and the dendrite of another neuron meet is called a synapse.

Chemical messengers called neurotransmitters relay messages across the synapses between neurons. Many problems in

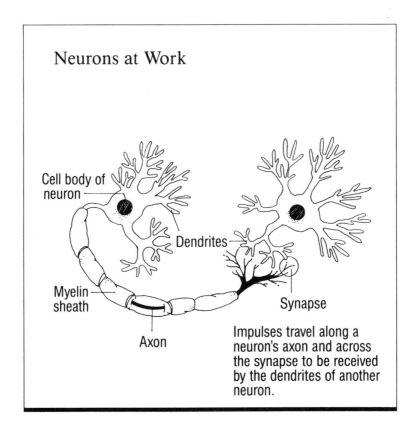

Neurons at Work

Cell body of neuron

Dendrites

Myelin sheath

Axon

Synapse

Impulses travel along a neuron's axon and across the synapse to be received by the dendrites of another neuron.

thinking and behavior seem to be related to improper or inefficient functioning of these neurotransmitters. For example, attention deficit hyperactivity disorder (ADHD) seems to occur when certain neurotransmitters are not doing the job they are meant to do. It is estimated that over a million children in the United States have this disorder, which can make it difficult for them to stay focused and pay attention in class.

CARE AND FEEDING OF THE BRAIN • If a baby's head had to be big enough to hold an adult brain, the baby could never be born. The wonderful solution to this problem is that the skull is soft when we are born, to enable us to fit through the birth canal. Then the brain begins to grow. During a child's first year of life, the brain will triple in size. As it continues to grow, it quickly runs out of room in the skull. Now the young child's relatively smooth brain begins to develop wrinkles. As the child grows and the brain takes in more information, it develops many wrinkles and folds, increasing its surface area without taking up much more space. By about the age of seven, the human brain weighs about as much as it ever will, about 3 pounds (1.3 kilograms).

Many things can interfere with the growth and development of the brain. Injuries to the brain can be from external sources (a blow to the head, a bullet or sharp object that pierces the skull) or internal (drugs or other toxic substances in the bloodstream). It only makes sense to protect your brain from injury—external or internal.

Taking care of your brain includes feeding it right. The food you eat can affect the chemical operation of your brain and thus the way you are able to use your mind. This means that the things you eat have an impact on your ability to think and learn.

The brain is nourished by certain substances in the blood. These substances come from the food you eat. For example, the brain relies on glucose for energy. Glucose is a sugar made from carbohydrates. When you eat food rich in carbohydrates, your body converts that to glucose, and the glucose is then available in the blood that flows to the brain.

Since glucose is a sugar, you might think that eating sugary foods should be good for the brain. But it's not. Eating sugar causes your body to produce insulin. The presence of insulin reduces the amount of glucose in your bloodstream. Thus too much sugar leads to too little glucose, which means a reduced food supply to brain cells. This can lead to crabbiness, poor concentration, tiredness, and other symptoms that make thinking and learning difficult.

Carbohydrates are good food for the brain. So are proteins. Proteins are broken down into amino acids. Many of the neurotransmitters that are so important in the firing of messages from neuron to neuron are either amino acids or are made from amino acids.

Vitamins are also necessary to an efficiently functioning brain. Vitamin A is crucial for the development of vision. It helps the process by which your eyes send information to the brain. Vitamin E helps the circulation of oxygen in your blood to the brain.

The proper feeding of the brain also includes avoiding the ingestion of harmful substances. Always wash fresh fruits and vegetables to remove such toxins as pesticides and other chemical pollutants. Try to avoid heavily processed foods that contain numerous chemical additives. And you're probably well aware of the danger to the brain posed by alcohol and illicit drugs. Even certain legal drugs, such as caffeine and nicotine, affect the brain and are best avoided.

The study of the proper feeding of the brain and body is a complicated science. Luckily for us, that age-old standard of eating a well-balanced diet with plenty of fresh fruits and vegetables still holds as a good rule of thumb. And nutritionists emphasize that a good breakfast is important if you want your brain to be ready to perform efficiently throughout the day. Studies show that children who don't eat breakfast (or who eat nonnutritious foods for breakfast) are less able to concentrate on schoolwork. They're hungry, and they're thinking about food. Their brain cells are hungry too!

You can receive someone else's heart or liver and still be you, but not someone else's brain. It just makes sense to take care of it.

PERCEPTION: THE FIRST STAGE OF LEARNING

In a way, the senses are the gateways to the mind. It is through our eyes and ears primarily, and sometimes through the other sensory organs (nose, mouth, skin), that we receive information about the world.

From the sensory organs messages are sent to the brain. These are sensations. What happens to these messages in the brain determines how we deal with the world. The result of this interaction between senses and brain is perception. Perception is the process by which we gain information about what exists around us.

Perception offers a good example of how genetics and experience interact. Our perceptions are molded by both the physical capabilities of our sensory receptors (as determined by our genes) and our past experiences.

FROM SENSATION TO INTERPRETATION • Babies are able to perceive many things very soon after birth, and this ability grows constantly. Within the first hours of life, a baby will turn its head to the left in response to a sound from the left, and turn its head to the right in response to a sound from that direction.

As the nerve cells in the perceptual system grow and increase in number, a baby can take in and make sense of

A baby's understanding of the world is based on what he or she perceives through the senses.

increasing amounts of perceptual information. Babies still are limited in their understanding of the world by what they can immediately perceive with their senses. By about one year of age, though, a baby starts to use memories and expectations to control behavior and begins to rely less on perceptions.

As we get older, we add information from memory to what we perceive in order to make decisions about what is happening around us. We add the past to the present. We also learn to anticipate the future. Thus our understanding of the present is not limited to our perceptions, as it is for a baby. We begin to rely on other sources of information besides just our senses to learn about the world. It is not the information sent to our brain from our senses that changes. What changes is our ability to interpret this information.

The mind gives meaning to what we see. Thus what anything "is" depends partly on who is looking at it.

Imagine yourself in class, listening to the teacher. There is a knock on the door and a man enters, dressed in a sports uniform. He hands the teacher a stack of booklets, says something to the class, and then leaves. Then the teacher asks the class to take out paper and write a description of what just happened. What kind of uniform was the man wearing? What color was his hair? His eyes? Was he short or tall? What did he say? Do you think that all the descriptions will be the same? Everyone saw and heard the same thing, right?

Well, yes and no. The visual and auditory stimuli were the same for everyone. But different people's abilities to receive sensory input vary, and what happens to that input once it is received varies even more.

How can two different people see the same thing and each say something different about what happened? This happens because a perception is seldom "pure"—that is, untouched by "thinking." Almost immediately upon perceiving something, your mind goes to work, associating it with other perceptions, labeling it, judging it, perhaps altering it.

Have you ever been fooled by your senses? You probably have. You think you see (or touch, taste, or smell) one thing, and it turns out to be something entirely different. You are dependent on your senses and your mind as you try to determine what is real because what you see isn't just what's there. It's what your mind does with what's there. This is why there is always at least some discrepancy between reality and perception, and between different people's perceptions of reality.

The more complicated the input, the more likely that perceptions will differ. If there were two men in the previous example instead of one, and they were wearing two completely different kinds of uniforms, and carrying different kinds of things, and said different things at the same time, there would probably be even more variation in the descriptions your classmates wrote.

SEEING IS BELIEVING • Of all our senses we normally rely on vision the most. Over half of our informational inputs come to us through our eyes. The retina "sees" spots of light and color. These patterns of light are relayed to the brain. The occipital lobe converts these dots into the images that we "see."

What we see and what is before our eyes are not necessarily the same thing. Vision is more than just receiving information about light and color; it includes what the brain does with this information. Vision requires eyes and brain. Your brain is therefore part of your visual system.

When babies learn to creep and crawl, and practice these skills, they are doing very important work. They are training the eyes and brain to work together in ways that will influence their ability to read, write, and perform tasks at arm's length—which is just about everything we do.

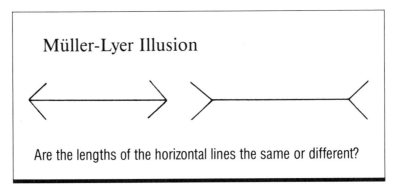

Müller-Lyer Illusion

Are the lengths of the horizontal lines the same or different?

MIND GAMES • There are many different illusions that show how your sensory receptors and your brain try to make sense of the world. An example of this is the Müller-Lyer illusion shown on this page. Although the two lines are exactly the same length, the one with the arrows pointing out appears to be shorter than the one with the arrows pointing in. This is because we tend to see objects in relation to other things and the space around them. In this case, the "other things" are the arrows, and they make us think that the lines are of different lengths.

Did you know that your eyes have a blind spot, a place with no receptors for receiving visual input? This should mean that when you look at the world there should be a tiny blank spot where you see nothing. The reason this doesn't happen is that your brain fills that spot in with what it sees around it. That is, the brain assumes that the spot is not going to be too different from its surroundings and blends it in. The brain is constantly making these kinds of assumptions about the world around it. It fills in details that aren't actually there. And sometimes it ignores information that *is* actually there. These assumptions are made by the brain to help it deal with a world in which there are sometimes too many and sometimes too few inputs. They greatly affect the way we perceive the world.

Two ways that your mind and your sensory organs can block perceptions are habituation and adaptation. In habituation, the sensory organ still sends the necessary signals, but the brain chooses to ignore at least some of them. This is what happens when you're thinking of something else while the teacher is talking. Your ears are still picking up the auditory signals and sending those messages to the brain, but the brain is ignoring them (because you've chosen to concentrate on something else).

Adaptation is when the sensory receptors themselves get used to a particular stimuli and as a result send fewer messages to the brain. If you have to go in a barn on a hot summer day when numerous pigs and cows and horses have been doing their thing, you're going to notice a strong odor right away. The receptors that handle your sense of smell will be firing off messages to your brain like mad. But if you stay in that barn long enough, the receptors will gradually slow down, sending fewer messages to your brain. As a result the smell won't seem so strong after a while; the sensory receptors will have adapted to it.

THE NEED TO PERCEIVE • All the knowledge that we hold in our minds initially came to us through perception. Without perceptions the mind would be cut off from the world outside the body.

Experiments in total sensory deprivation show that we cannot be healthy human beings if we are cut off from all sensory input. Sensory input gives us perceptions. Perceptions lead to thoughts. We have a basic need to experience, perceive, and think.

We are dependent on our senses for messages, for information. Without this information, there can be no learning, no thinking. This is why perceptions are the first stage of learning. Perhaps you can see now why enhanced perceptual skills can enhance thinking skills. If you want to be a better learner and thinker, start by being a better perceiver.

3

LEARNING: THE PROCESS OF UNDERSTANDING

What is learning? Is it something that *only* happens at your desk at school? (Does it *even* happen at your desk at school?) It most certainly is not. Whether you know it or not, whether you like it or not, you are involved in the process of learning a great deal of your waking time.

Whenever you are receiving sensory input, you are engaged in learning. What your mind does with the messages it receives is learning. When you listen to the words of a song on the radio, you are learning. You are receiving a message about love or hate or whatever the song is about. Whether you decide you like the song or not, whether you agree with the message it presents or not, your mind does something with the input. That something might be called encoding, a computer term for putting a message into code. It can also be called learning.

When you watch TV, even a situation comedy or violent movie, you are learning. But whether you are learning something positive or worthwhile is another matter. Studies have shown that children who watch a lot of cartoons and violent TV shows tend to choose violent solutions to problems more frequently than those who do not watch such shows. Apparently, that is what they've "learned."

*We think of learning as something that takes place
at school, but in fact it goes on all the time.*

Learning is something that happens inside you. It is personal. *You* are at the center of *your* learning process. Learning should help you understand the world as it really is, and help you cope with it.

PROGRAMMED TO LEARN • Learning is a natural process. We have a built-in drive to learn. It is human nature to want to understand the world. It is something your mind is programmed to do. From the moment of your birth, and possibly even before, you have been learning.

Think of all the amazing things you've learned to do already—walk, talk, read, write, add, subtract, and a long list of other skills. These might not seem so amazing now because you've learned to do them all, probably very well. But a lot of brainpower went into the learning of each of those skills. Author Robert Fulghum says, "Most of what I really need to know about how to live and what to do and how to be I learned in kindergarten."[1] And he does have a point. By the time we've reached the age of five or six, when "formal" learning usually starts, we've learned a great deal of important information. But as important as it is, the kind of learning we did as babies and young children is not enough to get us through life in the real world.

Our capacity to learn and the information available to be learned are both unlimited. We spend our childhood and adolescence slowly and carefully building an understanding of the world around us, trying to make sense of our experiences. When we go to school we learn new information, and ideally, we also learn skills that help us to use our natural learning ability better. This is what learning how to learn is all about—learning how to make the best use of our meaning-making machinery. If schools do a good job, we learn how to learn better, often without even knowing that that's what we're doing.

THEORIES OF LEARNING • What do a dog, a pigeon, an ape, and a playroom full of children have in common? They are all subjects of famous studies about learning. Scientists and psychologists have tried for years to figure out how learning happens. They have developed lots of theories about learning. Most of these theories can be classified as either behaviorist or cognitive.

Behaviorists believe that the way to study learning is to study behavior. They say that learning is behavior that results from specific stimuli. For example, hunger is a stimulus. Whatever an animal does to get food is behavior. When an animal develops a behavior that will consistently result in getting food, learning has taken place.

According to behaviorists, learning is basically a stimulus-response reaction. Learning can be improved by adding rewards and punishments. It is usually best for the reward to occur as close to the response as possible. And the reward should be neither too great nor too small.

By rewarding certain behaviors, you can teach animals many things. The Russian behaviorist Ivan Pavlov discovered that dogs learned to salivate at the sound of a bell if the sound was consistently followed by food. This kind of learning is called conditioning; the dogs were conditioned to associate the bell ringing with food.

Puppies learn to let you know when they need to go outside. With proper training they can learn to sit up and roll over on command. Chimpanzees can be taught to dress themselves and to communicate in limited ways. Animals can even be taught nonsense things—for example, pigeons can learn to peck keys on a piano in return for food.

Behaviorists believe that the same rules of learning apply to humans. They tend to see the young child as a blank slate, learning as a reaction to the environment. Behaviorists would say that your actions are the result of the consequences of previous behavior. You learn to do or not to do something based on what happens when you do it. This is often true. You can probably think of many times when you learned something because of a promised reward or threatened punishment.

Whether they know it or not, your parents and teachers have probably used behaviorist theories with you (for example, by rewarding good grades on your report card). What's important for you to know is that you can use conditioning on yourself. For example, if you want to lose weight, break a bad habit such as nail-biting or smoking, or learn a new skill such as piano playing, you could reward yourself for behavior that brings you closer to your goal.

People do learn some things as a result of rewards and punishments. But in people there are also higher mental processes that override such conditioning. People sometimes make decisions that defy the promise of reward or threat of punishment. Behaviorist theory can teach us a lot of good things about learning, but there is much that is learned that behaviorism cannot account for.

That is where cognitive psychologists come in. They are not necessarily in disagreement with behaviorist psychologists. But they tend to emphasize different aspects of the complicated processes of learning.

Cognitive psychologists believe that learning is a mental process. It's more about what takes place inside you than just a matter of what's happening to you. They might describe the young child as a seed, with all the components to create a full-grown plant tucked inside, waiting for the right time and conditions to grow and bloom. According to this theory, learning is a natural part of the brain's maturation.

Wolfgang Köhler, a cognitive theorist, once observed an ape in a cage trying to reach some bananas that were just beyond its reach. After a while, the ape "suddenly" figured out how to create a tool to reach the bananas. Köhler used the term "insight" to refer to the seemingly sudden ability to understand a relationship between things. He believed that the information on reward and punishment that the behaviorists had given us was all well and good, but that many animals, and certainly people, were capable of more complex styles of learning as well.

Jean Piaget, a psychologist who observed children, developed a theory that has been very helpful in understanding the complicated process we call learning. According to Piaget, all children go through certain stages of mental development in a specific order, although the rate at which children pass from one stage to the next may vary. Each stage builds on the one before. Piaget's stages are like roadside mile markers along the path of mental development. They indicate how far the child's mind has come.

A baby first learns by touching and moving, by using its senses and motor abilities. In other words, a baby learns by playing. A child with lots of good play experiences that encourage touching and moving is getting the best head start on learning.

Years of observation led the psychologist Jean Piaget, seen here late in his career, to conclude that children go through distinct stages of mental development.

At first, babies can know about only what they can see and touch, only what is right here right now. It is usually after about a year that they understand that something still exists when they cannot see it. (They go looking for an object that has disappeared, like a ball that has rolled behind a chair.) This is a sign that they are gradually moving into the next stage.

Between the ages of two and seven, the child learns to talk and use numbers. Because words and numbers are symbols for things (the word "cat" isn't a cat, it's a symbol for a cat), the child can now start to think about things that he or she can't (at the moment) see or touch. Language gives the child a tool with which to think. Other symbol systems include music, drawings and other art forms, and gestures. A child gradually learns about concepts like time and quantity, space (and spatial relationships like in front of, in back of, and so on) and causality (if I do this, that will happen).

The child who reaches school age gradually moves into the next stage and learns to use symbols (words) to perform mental operations (think). The child can think about things that cannot be seen, but they still have to be things that could be seen if they were there. At this stage the child can't yet think very well about abstract concepts.

The child can understand more now than before, however. For example, if you show a small child a short, wide container of liquid, and then pour the liquid into a tall, narrow container, the child will probably think that the narrow container has more liquid since it is filled higher. Until about the age of six or seven, most children are not able to understand the principle of conservation—that is, that the amount of liquid stays the same no matter what the size of the container. Piaget would say that it is ridiculous to expect a young child to understand this. The young child's brain just isn't ready to process this kind of information.

Children enter the last stage at about the age of eleven or twelve. Now the individual can think about abstract concepts— concepts such as thinking and learning. That is why you can understand what this book is all about!

The work of Piaget has had a great influence on the way we think about learning. We learned from him that the mind works at its own pace. We learned that children are ready to learn different things at different times in different ways.

For very young students, just coming out of the sensory-motor stage, lots of opportunities for touching and handling are important. That is how they learn. As children get older, they are expected to learn more easily with their eyes and ears. But

good teachers will still provide opportunities for physical activity, and good learners will find ways to keep all their senses involved in the learning process.

The more of your senses you can involve, the better your learning will be. The primary senses of learning are seeing (which includes reading), hearing, and touching (which includes working with things). Many times we use these senses in combination without even thinking about it. When your teacher brings in a filmstrip or video for you to watch, you are seeing and hearing. When your teacher demonstrates problems on the blackboard, you are seeing and hearing. When you perform a science experiment in class, or work on a group project, you are seeing, hearing, and touching.

LEARNING STYLES • Researchers from many fields have looked at the different ways people learn. Many of them agree that there are four basic learning style groups.[2] They are shown in the illustration on page 38.

Someone whose learning style of choice is number 1 is a feeling/watching person. People in this group tend to seek meaning in everything they do. They want to know why. They like to work one-on-one with other people. They like to understand the emotions involved in a situation and tend to be sympathetic listeners.

Someone whose learning style is number 2 is a watching/thinking person. These are the people who generally do best in traditional school settings. These people like details and accurate information. They like things to be orderly and to follow rules. They tend to be persistent and hard-working.

Which beaker contains more liquid?
Young children have difficulty
understanding that the short, wide
container holds the same amount
as the tall, narrow one.

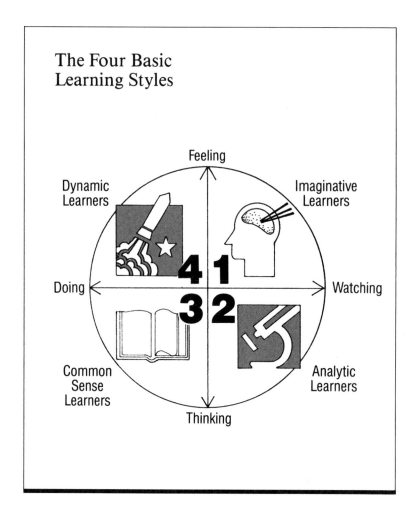

The Four Basic Learning Styles

Feeling

Dynamic Learners

Imaginative Learners

Doing

Watching

Common Sense Learners

Analytic Learners

Thinking

A person with a number 3 learning style is a thinker/doer. He or she wants to get information and then do something with it. These people tend to be practical and efficient. They want to make things happen.

An individual with a number 4 learning style is a feeler/ doer. These people often act on their instincts—they go with their gut feelings about things. They tend to be very imaginative and perhaps dramatic. They enjoy discovering things for themselves, and they want to know "what if." These people often have trouble in a strict "sit still and don't touch" school atmosphere.

It is very interesting to think about these learning styles, and it can be fun to see the style that "fits" you best. It can be helpful too—you can see why you might have trouble if your learning style and your teacher's teaching style are opposites. But the important thing about learning styles is to see them as a starting place, not an end point.

It's not enough to know your favorite learning style and then stay with it. The complete learning process includes all four styles. To be an effective learner you must move around the cycle, using the strengths of all four styles.

Other researchers say that people use five different learning "modalities." In this sense, the term "modalities" refers to the senses we use to receive and send messages. The five modalities are:

- *Visual learning.* Learners who use this modality like learning that involves "pictures." This would include charts and maps that illustrate concepts.
- *Auditory learning.* These learners like the sound of words; they like to have plenty of verbal explanations.
- *Kinesthetic learning.* These learners would rather do than talk. They like to use their hands and bodies.
- *Print-oriented learning.* These learners are good at storing ideas from the printed page. They like to read.
- *Group interactive learning.* Learners using this modality enjoy activities with others.

You can probably pick out one or two or three of these modalities to best describe the way you like to learn. That's fine. It's good to realize where your strength is. Use it to your advantage.

But don't limit yourself to one style of learning. Ideally, we should try to strengthen our ability to learn in as many different ways as possible.

One of the learning modalities that we are all required to use is the print-oriented learning style—reading. Reading is one of the most important skills for learning. For most of us, a large percentage of what we learn comes to us through reading. For adults who continue to learn after leaving school, reading provides the greatest tool for learning. People who don't read or who read very little are not making use of an important vehicle for learning.

THE COMPLETE LEARNING PROCESS • Regardless of what style of learning suits you best, or what style a situation seems best suited for, there are a number of characteristics that can be found in the complete learning process.

Ideally, the learning process should include decoding, input, synthesis, output, and feedback.

Decoding is the process of getting an overview of the subject. It lays the groundwork for learning. When you begin with a general idea of what you'll be learning about, you have a structure on which to hang new information. One of the best things you can do for yourself when starting a new class is to look through the textbook from start to finish. Take note of the chapter titles, the bold headings, the photo captions. Then, as you move through the course work, you'll have an idea of how today's material relates to other material in the course. When you have this general overview of the subject in your mind, you'll find that the details fall into place more easily.

Input is the actual content of the lesson. You get it when you listen to the teacher and when you read the textbook. This is the stage where paying attention really counts. Eliminate distractions as much as possible.

Synthesis takes place when you have the opportunity to think about the lesson. It involves relating the new material to other things you know.

Learning Through Reading

Here are four ways to make your reading more efficient, so that you can truly learn and remember more of what you read:

1. Read with a purpose in mind. Know why you are reading something (and just because the teacher told you to doesn't count). Is it to help you to understand something better? Know what that something is. This will be a big help in boosting reading comprehension.

2. When reading textbooks, take a glance first at headings, bold print, and anything else that stands out from the text. These items are clues to what you're going to be reading about, and previewing them will help you to stay focused. After reading a section, glance back at the items and see if you did in fact learn about them.

3. Often, first and last sentences of paragraphs contain the most important points. It might be a good idea to pay special attention to them. But don't try to get away with reading *only* the first and last sentences! You'd miss a lot of information that way.

4. The speed with which you read can be an important factor in being able to understand and remember material. By reading more quickly, you can increase comprehension by shortening the delay between words.

Output is an activity you perform with what you learned. Writing a report, taking a test, discussing a concept with a teacher or friend—these are examples of learning output.

Feedback comes as a response to your output. You get a grade on your report or test. Your teacher or friend engages in conversation with you. Feedback provides an opportunity to evaluate what you've learned and can be a springboard for further learning.

We learn best when we follow all the steps in the process. If you go right to input without decoding first, you are short-changing yourself. And if you stop at input, the learning will not be as effective as it could be. This is one of the reasons why television is a limited teaching tool. Even when the content of a TV program is good, it is basically "input" only; it generally allows for very little human interaction.

IMPROVING YOUR LEARNING ABILITIES • There are ways to boost your ability to learn. Generally, these involve taking advantage of the way your mind works.

• *Have the right attitude.* Learning is easier when you approach it in a positive manner. A confident attitude is also a plus. Good learners have confidence in their ability to learn.

• *Try to be interested and involved.* Material that is interesting to you will be easier to learn. Associating with other people who are interested and enthusiastic can help you develop this attitude, but there are lots of ways to make a subject you have to study more interesting. Using your imagination can make it fun. See if you can make a game of the material to be learned. Compete against yourself or a friend. You learn best when you are as actively involved in something as possible. It is up to you to get yourself involved.

• *Find a way to make the material meaningful.* Material that is relevant to you will also be easier to learn. Look for connections between this material and other subjects that interest you. For example, if you're trying to study a foreign language, imagine yourself in that country. Picture yourself in situations where knowing the language would be helpful.

• *Have a goal in mind.* Then you'll be able to tell when you've accomplished something, and that will be very rewarding. Measure improvements toward your goal.

• *Give yourself the best working conditions possible.*
Avoid distractions. If you are tired, hungry, or uncomfortable,
you will be fighting these internal distractions for your brain's
attention. The same goes for such external distractions as too
much noise, bad light, or temperatures that are too hot or cold.
Do what you can about these conditions, and then get on with
the task at hand. Don't let them stop you from getting the job
done!

• *Persevere and practice.* Notice what works and what
doesn't. Consult with others but don't let them take over. Good
learners don't give up easily. When they make a mistake or get
stumped by something, they back up and start again, maybe
from a different direction.

If what you're doing happens to be fun, it doesn't mean you
aren't learning. The saying "No pain, no gain" does not have to
apply to learning. In fact, your best learning will take place
when you are having fun. And learning of this kind may actually
be good for you. Researchers are exploring the possibility that
stress-free, joyful learning may give a boost to your immune
system. One of the best ways to stay healthy might just be to get
turned on to learning!

When you can see that the material to be learned is relevant to you, when you are interested in learning and growing,
when you are feeling positive mentally and feeling good physically, learning generally follows.

Learning should be developmental. That is, it is a continuous process, without an end. What you learn today connects
with and builds on what you learned yesterday. Almost everything you do takes into account things you've learned before.
And what you learn in the future will depend on what you learn
today. The average person acquires an incredible amount of
knowledge over the course of a lifetime.

LEARNING FOR UNDERSTANDING • Learning should be more than
just the gathering of new information. It should increase your
understanding of at least some aspect of the world. Learning

without real understanding is only partial learning. You may learn the facts well enough to pass a test, but do you understand the information well enough to apply it in a slightly different situation? In math, you might learn how to "plug" numbers into formulas for a math test, but when faced with a situation such as trying to figure out how much wallpaper you'll need for a room, will you know which formula to apply?

According to author Howard Gardner, there are really three stages of learning: the natural learning you do on your

---

Finding Time for Homework

Managing time is an important part of the learning process, especially as it relates to homework. Have you ever heard someone say, "Christmas really came early this year?" Christmas always comes on December 25! And yet many people get caught in a last-minute rush because they don't manage time efficiently.

It's much the same with homework assignments. When something's due "sometime next week," that sounds so far away that we don't do anything at all—until all of a sudden "sometime next week" is tomorrow! But when your teacher gives you a couple of weeks to do an assignment, it is probably because you are going to need that much time to do it well.

The two secrets to time management are (1) plan, and (2) start. Some people are very good at the first part. They plan and plan but never really get started. Others jump right in without stopping to think about the best way to go about the project. If you get in the habit of asking yourself if you are making the best use of your time *right now*, you will be on your way to using time more efficiently.

On Doing Assignments

1. Be sure you understand the assignment. Be sure you understand the words and concepts that are part of the assignment. Can you answer the question, "What am I supposed to do?" If you can't, find out, or you're in trouble before you've even started.

2. What does the teacher want from this assignment? How will it be evaluated? What is it going to take to get a good grade? What are the minimum requirements?

3. What do *you* want from this assignment? How will you know that you've learned something? Is it worth it to you to exceed the minimum requirements? How can you do this?

own as a child, the traditional learning you generally do in school, responding in programmed ways to teacher requests, and the skilled or expert learning you exhibit when you have mastered basic concepts, when you show that you understand by being able to apply learning.

It is possible to be an expert learner in certain subject areas while still in school. But some people never reach this level of learning. They never go beyond performing in expected ways. They never really understand what they've been taught and seldom use the resources of information at their disposal. But for those who learn for understanding, new worlds of thought and action are opened up.

In other words, learning should make you wiser. Abraham Lincoln once said, "I don't think much of a man who is not wiser today than he was yesterday." Are you wiser today than you were yesterday?

MEMORY: THE WORKSHOP
OF THOUGHT

Memory is involved in nearly all mental activities. Memory is our system for filing the things we have perceived and learned, our storehouse of things to think about.

Memory, learning, and thinking are very closely connected. Without memory, there can't be learning. Can you really say that you've learned something if you can't remember it? And memory is used constantly in all thinking processes. It has been called the workshop of thought.

Memory is a huge information storage system. Even if you don't think of yourself as having a particularly good memory, you can remember a remarkable number of things. John Griffith, a mathematician, believes that over the course of a lifetime, the average person's brain accumulates about five hundred times as much information as is contained in the *Encyclopaedia Britannica*.[3] That's a lot of information to work with!

FOUR CATEGORIES OF MEMORY • Memory is commonly broken down into four categories. The first category is called recognition. This means that you are able to recognize someone or something you've seen before. Recognition is the most basic kind of memory. It is an ability we are born with. Even babies are able to "recognize" the faces of those they see most often. This is the kind of memory used on multiple-choice tests.

The second category is called recall. Recall involves the repetition of acquired knowledge or the demonstration of a skill. Recall develops later than recognition because we have to be able to use symbols (words and numbers) to fill things in and recall them from memory. The ability of a one-year-old to understand that an object does not cease to exist when it disappears (as when a ball rolls under a chair) involves recall. This kind of memory is used in fill-in-the-blank tests, short essays, piano recitals, and such.

The third category is redintegration. Redintegration means being able to bring back a complex memory. This would be used in writing a long essay, or in remembering the sights, smells, sounds, and so on of a summer vacation.

The last category is residual memory. This refers to partial retention of a memory. You might remember that you went on a plane to visit your grandmother as a small child, but you don't remember anything that happened while you were there.

MECHANICS OF MEMORY • Scientists think that memories are created when neurons form more or less permanent patterns called "memory traces." These memory traces seem to be electrical impulses that spark certain chemical reactions, causing permanent changes in the brain. Exactly how this happens remains a mystery, although numerous researchers have spent their lives trying to figure it out.

Memory begins in your sensory receptors—information is momentarily held in your receptors. This is called sensory information storage. This information is then passed on to the part of the brain that stores short-term memory.

Short-term memory is very limited in the amount of information it can hold and the length of time it can hold it without reinforcement. For most people, seven items (such as the seven digits in a phone number) can be held only for a few seconds, perhaps a minute, if not repeated.

When something is placed in short-term memory, it will soon be gone unless something happens to move it into long-term memory. And it's a good thing. There are lots of things you only need to hold in your mind for a short time.

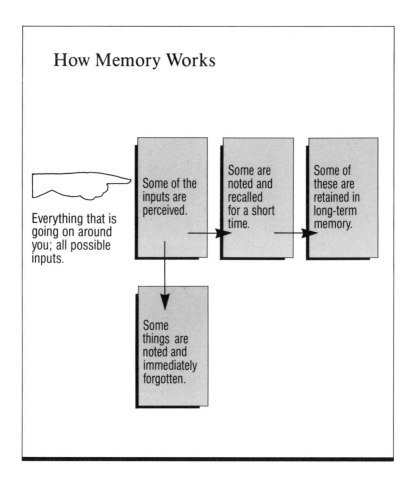

How Memory Works

Everything that is going on around you; all possible inputs.

Some of the inputs are perceived.

Some are noted and recalled for a short time.

Some of these are retained in long-term memory.

Some things are noted and immediately forgotten.

Think about how awful it would be never to forget anything. If you had to hold everything you ever knew in your conscious mind—the names of every classmate, every phone number you ever dialed, the words to every song, every commercial you ever heard—you'd probably go crazy!

But of course we do want to remember some things. These are the things we store in long-term memory. While short-term memory is very limited in the amount of information it can store, long-term memory can hold a virtually unlimited amount of information. Over time, however, some of the information stored in long-term memory can be lost (forgotten) or distorted.

Sometimes this happens within hours or weeks. Other memories will be stored for the rest of our lives.

Some things are learned and remembered after being heard or seen just once. But most of the time, information needs to be perceived more than once for it to be truly learned and easily remembered. Items of information seem to be retained best if they are associated with other things, are frequently used, or are very dramatic.

Most people who have studied memory agree that an environment free from interruption and distraction is important to improve memory. Loud music, ringing telephones, nearby voices raised in argument or conversation can all interfere with converting information from short-term to long-term memory.

Exactly where in the brain long-term memories are stored remains largely a mystery. It doesn't appear that specific memories can be lost by removing particular little bits of the brain. Portions of memories seem to be spread out over numerous areas. It may work something like a hologram, even a piece of which is capable of reproducing the whole picture.

We do know that the part of the brain called the hippocampus is involved in moving information from short-term to long-term memory. Scientists discovered this when an individual known as H.M. had his hippocampus surgically removed to end life-threatening seizures. H.M. could remember information that he'd learned before his surgery, but nothing that he'd experienced since. Think of what this means. This person could tell you all about the history of the United States that he'd learned as a child, all about President Roosevelt and World War II. But if you left the room and came back the next day, he wouldn't remember who you were or the discussion he'd had with you.

H.M. was unable to remember things because they were never put in his long-term memory. What about things that you know you learned, but you have difficulty remembering? After all, memory is a two-way street—input and output. We not only want information to go in efficiently, we want to be able to get it back out when we need it.

INFORMATION RETRIEVAL • Memories that are often called to mind seem to create pathways that make them easier to call up each time. Memories that are hardly ever used have a more difficult time coming into the conscious mind. And when we're upset, it can be even harder to call up memories. You may have experienced the phenomenon of test-day jitters, in which you let yourself get so worked up about taking a test that you can't remember information you are certain you know.

Emotions play a complicated role in memory filing and retrieval. Events tied to happy emotions are often easily remembered—an outing with a favorite relative, a day at an amusement park, falling in love for the first time, a first kiss.

So, if you want to remember something, fall in love with it! The great conductor Arturo Toscanini so loved music that he always remembered a piece after having performed it. He once wanted to perform a piece of music that he had conducted some fifty years before. Unable to find the score, he wrote down the notes as he remembered them. Later his memory of the music was compared to the actual score, and he had remembered every single note correctly. Toscanini's memory was so good because he was dealing with something he loved.

You probably find it easier to remember new information on subjects that you enjoy learning about, too. Conversely, sometimes events that are tied to extremely strong negative emotions become nearly impossible for a person to remember. This has been known to happen to victims of abuse or other forms of violence.

One of the keys to retrieving things from memory is multiple associations, or cross-referencing. Memories are interconnected. Each memory is stored in more than one way, and each memory is connected to many other memories. The more connections a memory has, the easier it will be to recall. It's as if the information were filed and cross-referenced under several headings, so that the mind has several ways to "look it up." For example, if Janet is your neighbor, is your friend, is in your class, and is on your sports team, it will be easier to remember her name than if she is only one of these things.

MNEMONICS • We can increase our ability to remember. Most people who want to remember things better learn to use one or more mnemonic aids. Mnemonics is the science and art of aiding the memory, and mnemonic aids are tools to help you do that. The following are some of the most popular mnemonic aids.

• *Mediators.* Mediators are physical cues. You pair something that you want to remember with some unusual physical cue. For example, you're on a bus and you want to remember to make an important phone call as soon as you get home. You take off one earring or switch your watch to your other arm, telling yourself that when you see your earring in your hand or your watch on the other arm you will be reminded to make that phone call.

• *Chunking.* Chunking involves grouping items together to make a list easier to remember. This is often done with numbers. For example, the number 894-23-1576 is easier to remember than 894231576. Another example of chunking would be to break up a shopping list—milk, bananas, butter, apples, cheese, chips—into three groups: milk, butter, cheese (dairy products); apples, bananas (fruit); and chips (other).

• *Music.* This is probably how you learned the ABCs. Remember when you had to start the song over from the beginning if you were interrupted in the middle? It's amazing what can be learned if put to a tune.

• *Rhythm and rhyme.* Rhythm and rhyme are similar to music. Many of us learned to remember the number of days in each month with the help of this poem:

Thirty days hath September,
April, June, and November.
All the rest have thirty-one
Except February, which has twenty-eight,
Except in Leap Year, when it has twenty-nine.

It's not even a good poem, but it works!

• *Acronyms.* An acronym is a word formed from the first letters of a series of words. Groups do this often, to make their names easy to remember. For example, Students Against Drunk Driving is known as SADD.

Encouraging Memory

1. Pay attention! The more closely you pay attention to a perception, the more likely it is that it will be recorded in your long-term memory and that it will be retrievable when you need it.

2. Make sure you understand the material. What you understand is more easily remembered than what you don't.

3. Make it meaningful to you. This will greatly assist your memory.

4. Reinforce the learning process. Read aloud. Now your ears and throat as well as your eyes and hands are involved. These activities involve different parts of the cortex, and the more parts involved, the stronger the memory will be.

5. Take notes. Another way you can reinforce the learning process is to write things down. Note-taking is an important part of the learning/memory process. The act of writing tends to leave a strong impression on the brain, making information easier to recall.

6. Review. Probably the most important part of the reinforcement process is review. The first review should occur shortly after the initial learning period. Short, frequent reviews thereafter are best. The more you review, the stronger your recall ability will be.

7. And then rest. Give your brain a chance to work over the information.

• **Acrostics.** An acrostic is formed by taking the first letter of each word in a list and making a sentence using words that start with those letters. One of the most famous examples is the sentence "Mary's violet eyes made John sit up nights pining," to remember the names of all the planets in our solar system in order from the sun (Mercury, Venus, Earth, Mars, Jupiter, Saturn, Uranus, Neptune, Pluto).

There are many additional practical systems for organizing information that help us to remember things.

For example, if you were asked to name all the states in the United States, it would be hard to do if you started naming them in random order. But if you used a system, such as alphabetical or geographic order, you would have a much better chance of remembering them all—assuming you knew them all in the first place! (You can't recall information your mind doesn't possess.)

With huge amounts of information bombarding us these days, skills in learning and memory are valuable to us all.

REVIEW • Only by periodically reviewing new material can you move information from short-term to long-term memory and make it easy to retrieve from long-term memory.

If you don't review, you're actually wasting the time and effort you put into learning new material because you probably won't remember as much or as well as you would if you reviewed. As you might guess, recall seems to be best immediately after a learning period, and then falls off quickly after this. Without review, about 80 percent of new material learned in a one-hour period will be forgotten within twenty-four hours.

Studies have shown that we recall more from the beginning and end of a study period than from the middle. So frequent, short study periods are better than one very long study period. Twenty- to fifty-minute learning periods seem to be best to meet the needs of understanding and recall.

People have their own internal rhythms, and different people are better at thinking and studying at different times of the day. Some people are "morning people," and they do their best work in the hours right after they wake up. Others are "night owls," and they do their best work in the evening and perhaps late into the night.

Whether you are a morning person or a night owl, you have to try to reach a balance between what seems to work for you and what is expected of you. For example, even if you are a "night person," you are probably expected to be in school between mid-morning and mid-afternoon.

Experiments seem to indicate that including some time for study and review just before going to bed may lead to effective learning, even for "morning people." Perhaps, after your conscious mind takes in information, sleep allows it to sink into your subconscious.

All this brings us to the subject of tests. Tests are part of the learning process. Teachers give tests to motivate you to learn and to measure what you have learned. Testing requires that you use your memory, but the purpose is to measure learning.

Taking Tests

- Know the material. Read and review.
- Know what kind of test it will be. You may study a little differently for a true-false or fill-in-the-blank test than you would for an essay test.
- Prepare your body as well as your mind. Get a good night's rest and eat a good (low in sugar) breakfast.
- Before starting the test, take a deep breath and tell yourself to relax. Don't clog your memory with stress.

The more you learn and remember, the easier it is to learn more, because you will have more knowledge in your brain for the new material to hook on to. And the more knowledge you hold in your brain, the more material you will have to think with.

THINKING: THE REAL WORK OF THE MIND

Most animals perceive and learn and remember, at least to some degree. Some animals even perform some thinking skills. But none come close to human thinking abilities. Nor can artificial forms of intelligence (that is, computers) think in the many marvelous ways that humans think.

Many of the things that you do for fun—performing in a band, going on a vacation, playing on a sports team—require that you plan, organize information, make decisions, and choose from alternatives. In other words, think!

Taking in facts and information is learning. Doing something with the information—integrating it with what you already know, and synthesizing it, creating new combinations of information—is thinking. Knowledge takes on power when thinking is applied to it. Thinking allows you to anticipate the future, expand on concepts, understand relationships, analyze, solve problems, imagine, explain, argue, and make judgments.

COGNITIVE DEVELOPMENT • The Greek philosopher Socrates taught young people to think by encouraging them to question and investigate, to form opinions of their own. He had no patience for people who accepted things just because that was the way they'd always been, or for people who merely repeated the words of others without really thinking for themselves.

Do schools today teach young people how to think? They usually don't teach thinking as a subject, but they hope that while you are learning "history" and "math" and "literature" you are learning to think. But learning how to think is different from learning specific subject matter.

Much of your education so far has probably required you to memorize facts and accept the thoughts of others rather than to do a lot of real thinking on your own. Usually, however, as you progress in school you are challenged to do more thinking. The sooner you get started with real thinking the better, because that's what will be expected of you in the "real world" after school.

The ability to think develops gradually. This development of thought is called cognitive development. It results from the continuous interaction between the abilities you are born with and the effects of your environment and experiences. Development of the ability to think depends upon development of the abilities to learn and remember. You can't think about things you haven't learned or can't remember.

To some extent, thinking develops naturally as the brain develops. The gradual increase in the ability to think is due (at least in part) to the growth and development of the brain. However, it is also true that experience and environment play a part in how well the brain and its thinking functions develop.

The development of language is also a key to the development of thought. The ability to use language has a lot to do with the ability to think. This is because the mind thinks mostly with words. Yes, sometimes we use mental images, but to communicate our thoughts to others we usually use words. Having words for our thoughts often enables us to think better. It would be very difficult to think very much without words. If you want to be a good learner and thinker, it helps to be good at using words.

NAMES, CATEGORIES, AND CONCEPTS • As children learn to use words, they begin to give things names. Naming words, like "dog," "ball," and "cookie," are usually among a young child's first words. After giving objects names, young language-

An eighteenth-century view of the Greek philosopher Socrates, who lived in the fifth century B.C. Socrates taught his students to think for themselves by encouraging them to question and investigate.

learners move on to placing named objects in categories. This is one of the most basic steps in thinking. Placing information in categories helps us to make sense of new information. "Chairs," "people," "food," and "toys" are all examples of categories.

As we develop and use categories, we have an idea of what the best example of the objects in a particular category should look like. Say the category is chairs. We can probably think of several examples of what "good" chairs look like. We can also think of some things that look different from that ideal, but still fit well enough into the category of chairs. And we can think of extremes—objects that are so far from the ideal example that they no longer fit in the category (for example, a chair that is so wide that it becomes a couch).

It takes time for a child to work out the details of what belongs in what category. The idea of subcategories in larger categories takes even longer. For example, a child learns that two animals called Inky and Tiger belong in the same category: cats. He learns that cats and dogs are different and belong in different categories. But cats and dogs can belong in the same larger category: animals. The fact that a cat, a dog, and a plant can belong in the same category (living things) is even harder to understand. A four- or five-year-old might understand this concept; a three-year-old probably would not.

Categorization helps a child know what to expect. All things in the category "dog" are expected to act in certain ways. It is hard work to convince a child (or a person of any age, for that matter) that they have miscategorized something.

From time to time, however, we need to re-sort the information in our minds and update our categories. The more appropriate and realistic our categories are, the more appropriately we will deal with the world around us. Even if we thought as a child that all creatures that swim are fish, we can learn that whales and dolphins belong in a different category.

Categorizing chairs and fish may not seem too difficult, but as you get older you learn more and more complex information. This learning is made easier when new information can be linked with old. One of the first things your mind does with new information is decide whether or not it "goes with" something you already know—whether it can be placed in a category. This way, each new bit of information does not need to be treated as something unique. When you learn something new, it is easier to think about it if it can be lumped with something you already know.

The danger of this, of course, is that you may treat information that really is unique and unlike anything you've ever seen before as if it is like something else. The best way to guard against this is to be aware of your categories. Don't be afraid to reevaluate and change them.

Categorizing can also lead to stereotyping and prejudice. Many times we want to put people into categories based on one characteristic. This is called stereotyping. Few people are "just like us" or "completely different from us." Few people are "all good" or "all bad," either. The truth is usually somewhere in between.

Everyone uses stereotypes, and sometimes stereotypes help you—they allow you to go into a new or unusual situation and apply some knowledge you've learned before. Sometimes stereotypes are neutral or positive. If you hold a stereotype that all ministers are caring and considerate, then this might help you seek the aid of such a person when you are in need of help.

But sometimes stereotypes can trip you up because they are oversimplifications. This is an important limitation to remember. If you had a bad experience with a certain person when you were a child (say, a person of a different race or of a particular occupation like policeman or teacher) you might continue to have a negative opinion of all people who fit in that category. This is where the need to reexamine your categories comes in. When you're dealing with, for example, a policeman, and feeling very negative toward this person, ask yourself if it is something this individual has done that is bothering you, or if it's the baggage you carry about people in this category. You should be prepared to discard a stereotype when it does not apply.

From categories we move on to concepts. The young child *knows* that it isn't fair for her to have two cookies and someone else to have six. She *learns* that it isn't fair the other way around either. She is developing a concept of fairness. As she grows and learns, she can expand this concept of fairness to include the many ideas that we hold about "justice," a larger concept.

Much of our thinking is shaped by these names, categories, and concepts. Often they are so much a part of us that we don't even know they're there.

MIND-SETS AND MIND TRAPS • All our categories and concepts make up what we call a mind-set. Your mind-set is the way you view the world based on your background and experiences. Your mind-set leads you to see things in a certain way and may make it difficult to be open to contradictory information.

Each person's mind-set is unique to that person because no two people have exactly the same background and experiences. Yet different people's mind-sets share common elements. It is the things our mind-sets have in common that allow us to communicate with each other.

Many things have affected the particular mind-set that you have developed and will continue to develop. These are the things that make you unique. They include:

- *Experiences.* No one has experienced everything, so our experiences are limited. Each person's set of experiences is unique.
- *Knowledge.* No one knows everything, so our knowledge is limited, too.
- *Mood.* The mood we're in can affect the way we think about things.

Much of what we call thinking relates to our use of the categories and patterns that make up mind-set. How well we think often depends on how much we are in control of pattern-using mechanisms, rather than being controlled by them. People who let their categories control them often fall into thinking traps.

For example, there is the problem that author Edward de Bono calls monorail thinking. Monorail thinking tries to make everything fit the mental set or ignores it altogether. It is not open to setting up new tracks. A monorail thinker reaches a conclusion and writes it in cement. That's it; the thinking's done; this is the way it will be forever. This narrow-minded thinking leads to what might be called mental fossilization or hardening of the categories. The best way to avoid becoming mentally fossilized is by careful attention to mental flexibility.

The opposite of monorail thinking is adaptive thinking. An adaptive thinker realizes that a conclusion is only a temporary point of view that can be reexamined and changed or abandoned as new information comes in. With monorail thinking you travel the same route and see the same sights over and over again. Adaptive thinking leaves you free to take different trains in different directions.

Rationalization is another mind trap. It's a way we fool ourselves—we explain things to ourselves in a way that will make us feel good, even if it isn't right. Rationalization helps us to avoid the mental pain of admitting we are wrong about something and saves us from having to change. It also keeps us from being open-minded. For example, if you made a nasty remark to a friend in the heat of an argument, you might tell yourself, "Well, she really is fat [or whatever] anyway," when you know that the right thing to do would be to apologize.

The way out of the rationalization trap is to realize that everybody does something wrong or stupid sometimes. Try to recognize when you've made a mistake—or when you're about to make one. Resist the urge to rationalize. Make a change. That will result in growth.

The best way to avoid making stupid mistakes and doing things that are wrong is to think before you act or speak; give your mind a chance to do its work.

LEFT BRAIN AND RIGHT BRAIN • You use thinking to solve everyday problems all the time. Obviously, it is to your benefit to become an effective thinker. Part of the secret to doing this involves getting your whole brain involved in the thinking process. In Chapter One you learned that there are two hemispheres in the brain, left and right. Research over the past several decades has shown that even though these two hemispheres look very much alike, they have different ways of processing information.

The characteristics of the two hemispheres can most accurately be visualized on a continuum, rather than on an either/or basis. In other words, when we're leaning more toward orderly, logical thinking, the left brain is in control. When we are being more emotional, more feeling-oriented, the right brain is in control. Most people shift from left-brain–dominant thinking to right-brain–dominant thinking and back again continually. And this is good—we should vary our thinking styles as situations change.

An EEG, which measures brain waves, can be used to show the different levels of activity in the left and right hemispheres during certain kinds of tasks. These waves seem to show the right hemisphere to be "quieter" while an individual is using verbal abilities (say, writing a letter) and the left hemisphere to be "quieter" while the individual is using spatial abilities (like arranging blocks).

The left hemisphere seems to deal best with words and numbers, so most of our language, mathematical, and logical thinking skills rely on the left hemisphere. The left side of the brain deals with the stuff that makes you smart by society's standards: numbers, dates, facts. The left brain likes to organize things in logical, sequential fashion. It follows schedules. It explains things.

The right hemisphere deals more with sensory data, like smells and sounds, and spatial qualities, like depth. The right side of the brain deals with emotions and intuition. Whereas the left brain dissects things and looks at detail, the right brain tends to look more at the "big picture."

The right brain is better at perceptual tasks. It is used in recognizing faces and familiar objects. It is better at seeing and understanding spatial relationships. It uses mental images, rather than words, as its language.

What do we mean by mental images and spatial relationships? Mental images are to the right brain what words are to the left. If you are good at seeing how the pieces of a jigsaw puzzle fit together, if you enjoy imagining how the furniture in a room might be rearranged, you are using mental images and spatial relationships. Other activities that rely heavily on mental images and spatial relationships are gymnastics, choreography, and sculpture.

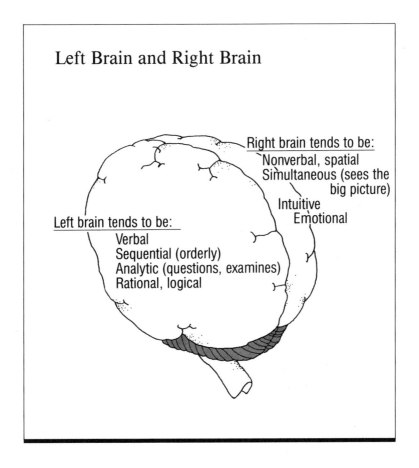

Left Brain and Right Brain

Right brain tends to be:
Nonverbal, spatial
Simultaneous (sees the
                big picture)
Intuitive
Emotional

Left brain tends to be:
Verbal
Sequential (orderly)
Analytic (questions, examines)
Rational, logical

The left brain thinks with words. The right brain thinks with images. Both think. And good thinking uses the whole brain. In fact, really good thinking uses the whole body, since mind and body affect each other so much.

Virtually all thinking skills work best when both the left and right hemispheres are acting in cooperation. This is where the corpus callosum comes in, letting each hemisphere know what is going on in the other. For example, the process of communication uses both hemispheres. While the left hemisphere controls the mechanics of speech, the right hemisphere is very involved with the need to communicate. In order to sing a song, you need the right brain to help you out with melody, pitch, and rhythm, and you need the left brain to work the vocal chords and remember the words. Your goal-oriented left brain can motivate you to get started and remind you to keep on task. Your emotional right brain can help you to have fun while you're at it.

The better we are at using both hemispheres, the better our chances of being complete, successful persons. Good thinking requires that we take advantage of and appreciate the capabilities of both sides of our brain.

Most great artists, scientists, and inventors have been "whole-brained" persons. Leonardo da Vinci is an example of a truly great whole-brained individual, one of the greatest minds of all times. The secret to using *your* brain more efficiently is not so much to use one side or the other more, but to use both sides of the brain, together, more often.

CRITICAL
THINKING

At school, at work, and at home, you're bombarded with information and with attempts at persuasion—in everything from television advertisements to conversations with your friends. How can you sort through these various appeals and reach rational conclusions? Critical thinking is a skill that can help.

Critical thinking is NOT negative thinking. Instead, it requires challenging your usual ways of thinking, and being prepared to learn some new ways.

Critical thinking is a two-part process. The first step is to examine or analyze a statement or belief. This includes identifying the assumptions and biases involved and separating fact from opinion. (Assumptions are things we accept as true; biases are opinions that may color the facts.) The second step is to consider the pros and cons of the situation—the negative and positive aspects—and to imagine and explore alternatives.

Taking these two steps will allow you to reach a conclusion based on rational thought. A conclusion reached this way is more than the sum of what you've been taught. It's what YOU decide about the inputs and experiences of your life.

Most people have done at least some critical thinking— they've examined some belief they've held, found it no longer appropriate, and replaced it with new information. If you're having trouble imagining yourself doing this, consider this question: Do you believe in Santa Claus? Did you believe in Santa Claus when you were a small child?

So, even though the concept of critical thinking may be new to you, it is something you have already done. But even though you've done it and continue to do it, you may not do it well. Some people do it more often, and better, than others.

What do people who are good at critical thinking do?

Critical Thinkers

- ask questions and listen attentively.
- try to get as much information as possible.
- consider pros and cons of each idea.
- reach conclusions after questioning, analyzing, and evaluating.
- are flexible and willing to change.
- are tolerant of diversity.

Critical thinkers are aware that unspoken assumptions underlie most statements. Critical thinkers are likely to question their own and other people's assumptions. For example, many commercials assume that you want to be just like everyone else. They show people doing something, and assume that that will make you want to do it, too.

A person using critical thinking skills takes note of other people's points of view and notices the prejudices and biases others exhibit. Critical thinkers are also aware of their own prejudices and biases. Everyone has them! A critical thinker tries to separate facts, which can be verified by consulting a variety of sources, from opinions, which reflect personal points of view.

One of the biases a critical thinker needs to be aware of is confirmation bias. This occurs when we pay attention only to facts that support our views and ignore those that don't. Thus we say that our position is confirmed. But nothing is really proved until you can show that there are no examples that disprove it. For example, if your horoscope accurately reflects what happens to you one day, you might say that it confirms your belief in astrology—conveniently ignoring all the days that your horoscope is wrong.

Critical thinkers are also able to get rid of old beliefs and actions when they prove to be no longer valid. This does not mean discarding old ideas just because they're old. Nor does the critical thinker accept or reject new information just because it's new. Critical thinkers take all information into consideration and reach a conclusion after questioning, analyzing, and evaluating it.

A critical thinker can justify actions because they are performed as the result of rational thinking. And yet anyone who uses this technique soon realizes that few real-life problems have simple, absolute answers and that some questions have no single answer. That is why critical thinkers are flexible thinkers. They are prepared to make changes when necessary.

Some people think that being "critical" means being negative, putting down the accomplishments of others. But true critical thinking is quite different from that. With critical thinking comes the understanding that virtually everything that you believe to be obvious or unquestionable could be considered bizarre by someone who happens to hold different beliefs. It also brings the understanding that most of the beliefs you have are the result of your experience, especially when and how you were born and raised. A critical thinker realizes the value of other people's beliefs and respects their opinions.

Critical thinking does not give you the right to insult or abuse another person. It's important to develop the ability to challenge a statement or an idea without putting down the person who expresses it—to question the statement, not the speaker. If you don't develop this skill, people will simply not

listen to you. And keep in mind that when you challenge others with your critical thinking skills, you can expect to be challenged in return, and you must be open to that as well.

CRITICAL THINKING AND ARGUMENTS • Maybe you're starting to see that critical thinking skills can be very useful in arguments. Such skills can help you develop and present your point of view, and they can help you develop rational arguments to challenge the statements of others.

Most arguments are best avoided. Very seldom does an argument change a person's mind. It usually causes those involved to dig into their positions and defend them at all costs. If one person appears to have won the argument, then the other will have lost. People don't like to lose. Instead of accepting the winner's point of view, the loser will probably resent the winner. So everybody loses.

But in the case where two opposing viewpoints do meet in confrontation, there are some things to keep in mind. First of all, stay calm. Try to keep focused on the problem at hand, not on the personality of the other person. Remember that you are not likely to change the other person's mind, and that the more you try to force your opinion, the more your opponent will resist. State your point of view as simply as possible. Listen to the other view. See if you have any common ground at all, if there is *anything* you agree on that you can work with.

When discussing an issue with someone you disagree with, it is good to try to understand his or her point of view. This does not mean you have to abandon yours. It just allows you to see people with whom you disagree as something more than "bad guys."

Students in a discussion group
debate a point. Critical thinking skills
can help you analyze the arguments
of others and present your own.

A technique called "think and listen" can be helpful in an argument. First one party gets a chance to talk, while the other listens. Then they switch. That way both get listened to. And there is power in listening as well as in being listened to.

Points to Remember in Arguments:

- Try to avoid thinking in "either-or" terms. There may be a whole range of possible solutions to examine.
- Be careful about drawing conclusions from material that is incomplete or taken out of context. Try to get the whole story.
- In an argument, beware of people throwing in things that are beside the point, or focusing on personalities instead of issues.
- Be aware of what techniques of persuasion are being used on you. Some people try to persuade you by appealing to your intellect. Others go right to your emotions.
- Be on the lookout for thinking traps. Watch out for people who use categorical statements. These are statements that relate information in a way that makes you feel as if there can be no argument. An example of a categorical statement would be "Everybody knows that all people who wear glasses are smart."
- Beware of the cause-and-effect trap. Just because one thing happens after another does not mean that the first thing causes the second.
- Beware of the numbers trap. Don't be swayed simply by statistics. They can easily be manipulated and there is generally more than one way to interpret them.

GARBAGE DETECTING • Probably one of the most common uses for critical thinking skills is in deciding whether to accept or reject things that people tell you. We might call this garbage detecting—learning how to detect and reject information that is wrong or inappropriate.

How do you know if what someone is telling you is the truth? Even people who might not always tell the truth—salesmen, politicians, advertisers—sometimes tell the truth, and there is usually at least some truth in most of what they say. And even people who mean to tell you the truth—teachers, parents, friends—may simply be wrong sometimes. Sometimes even common sense can be wrong. And the fact that a lot of people believe something does not necessarily make it true. It once seemed to make perfect sense that the Earth was flat and that the sun moved around it—and a lot of people believed that! Most of the time, untruths are passed on unintentionally by people who are confused, misinformed, or too accepting of information. Usually close observation and further research will lead to a correction of false conclusions.

Garbage detecting is hard enough when you are face to face with the people giving you information. It can be even harder when dealing with the media. The media include any-thing we get information from (TV, radio, newspapers, books). Since there's no way any of us can get all the information we need from people we talk to face-to-face, we rely on various forms of media to help us out.

You need to think critically about what you see and hear in the media. You must also realize that the various media may have various reasons for choosing what information they give. Are they giving all sides of the story? What aren't they telling you?

One way to increase the likelihood of getting a complete picture about something is to diversify your sources. Expose yourself to as wide a variety of sources as possible instead of relying on the same source of information all the time. By using critical thinking skills you can limit the amount of garbage information you accept. And remember the letters *GIGO*—*g*arbage *i*n, *g*arbage *o*ut.

MANY USES OF CRITICAL THINKING • Critical thinking skills can be helpful in arguments and in everyday garbage detecting. Can you think of other ways to employ critical thinking skills? How about in choosing friends and in maintaining friendships? Perhaps you might need to examine the criteria by which you choose your friends. Do you choose people with interests similar to yours? Or are material things, like clothes and money to spend, important factors?

Critical thinking should obviously be used when you are called on to vote for something or someone. What assumptions do you make about someone who'll be a good class president? What are your prejudices toward the candidates? What are the facts, as opposed to the opinions, regarding the issues involved? Weigh the positive and negative aspects of each candidate. Can you make a rational, critical choice? These same thought processes apply whether you are voting for class president or president of the United States. (The consequences of some choices, however, are obviously much more serious than others!)

We know that it is very difficult (if not impossible) for young children to be critical thinkers. Young children love to question, as anyone who has spent time around a two- or three-year-old will agree, but this isn't really a sign of critical thinking. The difference is that the critical thinker can analyze the response and decide whether to accept or reject information based on logical thought processes. The young child just keeps on asking questions.

Young children see things as yes or no, true or false, good or bad. But as we grow up, we are expected to learn that not everything in life is as simple as that. There are a lot of gray areas in between. There are many situations where there are alternatives to choose from, where there is more than one "right" or "wrong" thing to believe or do. We have to learn that reality may fall far short of dreams and expectations, and we can use critical thinking to help us deal with that.

As we reach adolescence and adulthood, and learn to think critically, we start to discard some of the beliefs we held in childhood that no longer apply. This is a continuous process that we will carry on as long as we are rational, intelligent beings. It is what brings us out of our past and into our future. It is part of becoming the best that we can be.

Critical thinking is a necessary skill for citizens of a democracy, and it can be said that it is a necessary skill for being a well-developed person. It is not just an abstract idea, something that happens in your mind and has nothing to do with how you act. It should be a major force in determining how you act.

Critical thinking is not a skill to save for classroom use only. It is an important tool in every aspect of your life.

7

CREATIVE THINKING

Creative thinking is related to critical thinking in that both are higher-level thinking skills that help us to use our minds effectively. But while critical thinking tends to be convergent, working from a great deal of information toward a best solution, creative thinking tends to be divergent, working from a bit of information toward many possible ideas.

Creative thinking requires creativity, the ability to produce something new. Producing something is at the heart of any good definition of creativity. Creativity is active; it produces.

Creativity requires the ability to see beyond mistakes, to be flexible, to be original. Creative thinking is not limited by the obvious and the ordinary. Creativity is often marked by unconventional thinking. Creativity is the opposite of conformity. To conform is to do what is expected. To create is to produce something new, something different. But true creativity is more than merely doing something different. It is doing something different for a purpose, in an effort to make an improvement.

Somewhere along the way, many people have gotten the idea that being different is bad. Being different is neither good nor bad all by itself. When creative energies are channeled into constructive programs, being different can be very good indeed.

Sometimes this divergent behavior is acceptable; sometimes it is not. Quite often, it is not welcome in a classroom. Because of this, many students may think that divergent or creative thinking is not important.

In real life, creative thinking is extremely important. It can make the difference between just getting by and being truly successful in life. It can be the factor that enables you to be happy, even when things in life are not going your way.

People who think and act creatively are sometimes looked on with suspicion because to be creative means to create new things and systems, and some people would just rather have the same old things and systems. But there are also many people who have become very successful by daring to be different, by daring to diverge.

All of us have the potential for creativity, and all of us have the need. Creative thinking is a skill that is handy for bank presidents and corporate executives, for auto mechanics and machine operators. It is useful for beauticians and teachers and journalists and artists.

Some people have a fixed idea (or stereotype) of what the creative person is like. But really, there is no such thing as "the creative person" and "the uncreative person." All people are creative. Some are better at creativity than others, but all are capable of it. For example, consider the personalities of the following individuals, two composers and two artists. All became famous for their creativity, but each was very different as an individual.

- Wolfgang Amadeus Mozart was known for his sense of humor. He enjoyed parties and practical jokes.
- Ludwig van Beethoven was proud and irritable, often difficult to get along with, especially as he got older.
- Vincent van Gogh was rough, emotional, and argumentative.
- Pierre Auguste Renoir was tender, compassionate, relaxed, and gentle.

Wolfgang Amadeus Mozart (left) and Ludwig van Beethoven (below) were both creative geniuses, yet they were opposites in personality. Mozart was known for his sense of humor, while Beethoven was often irritable.

However, although there is not a particular creative personality, some characteristics are commonly found among highly creative people. They tend to be hard-working people who do not give up easily. They are independent thinkers who want to find things out for themselves.

Neither age nor sex determines creativity. Men and women, the young, the middle-aged, and the old can be creative.

It is not necessarily true that the more intelligent a person is, the more creative he or she will be. Sometimes people who are *very* intelligent have trouble being creative because they may be too rigid in their learning and thinking style, and too self-critical. A certain level of intelligence is needed for creativity, however. Creative thinking depends on your storehouse of information (your memory) for raw materials for new ideas. Creativity is not making something from nothing—it is making something new from things you already know about. It is really hard to be creative without a foundation of knowledge to work with. (The same is true for critical thinking.)

Inventing the telephone was a stroke of creative genius. But Alexander Graham Bell was able to do this because he had knowledge of how the human ear works and of how electricity and magnetism work. He used his knowledge to create something new. History has shown that minds prepared with knowledge are more likely to be ready when inspiration hits.

THE CREATIVE PROCESS • According to most theories, there are four stages in the creative thinking process: saturation, incubation, illumination, and evaluation.

Saturation is information gathering, or research. Most of the work in school is saturation. Gathering and memorizing information is emphasized. This may not seem very creative, but to think up new and original ideas we must first be acquainted with the ideas of others. Information gathering prepares the mind to be creative.

Sometimes we get so involved with the saturation process that we almost forget about the other stages. It is important to

> ### The Stages of Creativity
>
> - Saturation. Preparation; gathering and absorbing information
> - Incubation. Stepping back; merging and integrating information
> - Illumination. Insight; the great *aha*!
> - Evaluation. Implementation and verification; developing and analyzing the creation

remember that information gathering is important when it paves the way for the rest of the steps in the creative thinking process.

After having saturated yourself with information about a problem, you may find that you need to walk away from it for a few minutes, or sleep on it for a night or two. By turning your conscious mind to other things you may allow the unconscious mind to go to work. This is the next step in the creative thinking process, incubation.

Incubation occurs largely outside the conscious awareness. It takes place in the mind (often in the right hemisphere) while you are doing something else. It may take only a few minutes, or it may take place over a much longer period of time. Either way, when a solution is reached or an idea formed, it is communicated to the consciousness, and this is illumination.

Illumination can occur in an instant, or it can be a slowly growing phenomenon. Have you ever said: "It just came to me"? This is illumination at work. But illumination or insight does not "come out of the blue." It is generally the result of a great deal of conscious and unconscious work.

The fourth stage of the creativity process, evaluation, might best be described as hard work. It is what you do with your creative ideas.

It is interesting to note that while we tend to think of creativity as a "right brain" activity, in fact the whole brain is involved. While divergent thinking and the ability to see patterns and relationships are typically right-brain activities, the first and the last step in the creative thinking process (saturation and evaluation) require left-brain, convergent thinking. Thus, even in creativity, whole-brain thinking is best!

INCREASING CREATIVITY • What can you do to help promote the creative process in yourself, to increase your ability for creative thinking?

Creativity seems to require a certain amount of "aloneness." This quiet time seems to help because it makes it easier for the unconscious to "speak up." Often this time alone is hard to find. Some people are afraid to be alone. Others may worry that people will think they're strange because our society values social contact, not solitude. Whether it's passive stimulation like radio or TV, or active stimulation like the company of

---

Helpful Hints for Creativity

- Don't neglect the saturation stage. Prime your mind with knowledge. This is where reading from a wide range of sources is valuable.
- Give yourself quiet time alone. Let your mind work over things.
- Act on your ideas. Give your creativity a chance by following through on creative thoughts.
- Engage in activities that allow your mind to work in creative ways. These include participation in plays, writing in a journal, and creating things with your hands.

friends or family, we are seldom alone and quiet. This makes it difficult to tap into the rich resource that is the unconscious mind.

Give yourself some alone time once in a while. This means taking time to do what others would call "doing nothing." When you are not physically active, you can devote your energy to internal thinking. Let yourself daydream a little.

But don't stop there. Once you've been alone, once you've taken some time to think, then it's time to act. As the old saying goes, "Creativity is 10 percent inspiration and 90 percent perspiration." All the good ideas in the world won't mean much if you don't take steps to put them in action. Creativity is imagination *plus* effort.

CREATIVE TECHNIQUES • One of the most basic tools for creative thinking is the brainstorming technique.

Brainstorming is something you can do by yourself or in a group. It is a technique for allowing open-ended creative thinking to take place.

If you are working by yourself, you have to be your own note-taker. Start with the first idea that comes to mind. Jot down whatever key phrases will help you remember that idea. Then move on to the next idea, and the next. Write down every idea that comes to mind, no matter how crazy or impossible it seems. Don't criticize any of your ideas at this point.

Rules for Brainstorming

- No criticism allowed.
- Quantity wanted—the more ideas the better.
- Originality wanted—wild, unusual ideas are good.
- Combination and improvement wanted—build on previous suggestions.

Keep going until you start to run out of ideas. Then go back and see if any of the ideas you've written down give you more ideas. In brainstorming it's good to build on other ideas, and crazy ideas may lead to really good ones.

When you've decided that you're through listing ideas, go back to the start and begin to narrow down the choices, highlighting the ones that are the best and eliminating ideas you really don't like. Before you decide that any idea is impossible,

Creative ideas often emerge from group brainstorming sessions like this one.

though, think about it for a minute. If it were possible, would it be a good idea? Is there anything that can be done to make it possible?

When brainstorming in a group, one person is appointed to take notes and write down every idea. No criticism of persons or ideas is allowed. Negative attitudes kill new ideas. It is OK for one person to create a new idea by building on another person's idea. Be sure to encourage everyone to participate.

You can increase the production of good ideas by keeping two things in mind: First, hold off judgment until you've come up with as many ideas as possible. Most people apply judgmental thinking too soon, stifling creativity. Second, the more ideas you think of, the better your chances of having at least one really good idea, if not more.

Another technique of creative thinking includes the use of analogy. When we use analogies, we make comparisons. We say that one thing is like another in some way. Then we think about how else the two things may be alike.

One method that includes the use of analogy is the theory of synectics, developed by William J. J. Gordon in the 1960s. Gordon's idea was for people to use analogies to make the familiar seem strange and the strange seem familiar. By pairing things in unlikely ways, he proposed, the mind could be opened to see things in new ways. He believed that people could increase their creative abilities by practicing synectics.

An example of this approach would be filling in blanks with an appropriate but unusual choice of words:

Eyes like_____

The fly buzzed like_____

Another example would be putting together two words that are opposites: tough love, sweet revenge.

Synectics has been used to solve problems in industry by getting people to approach problems from unusual directions. For example, instead of trying to think of a new kind of can opener, a work group was asked to think about the concept "openings." From this approach, new ways to open cans, such as the plastic pull tab on an orange juice can, were developed.

Creative Thinking Activities

- List as many uses for a pencil as you can.
- List all the things you can think of that are soft.
- List words that describe happiness.
- Close your eyes. List all the things you hear and smell.
- Write a letter as if you were a character in a book writing to another character in that book.
- Write a letter to a famous person in history. Then write that person's response.
- Create a picture using only letters or numbers.
- Think of something that needs to be invented. Describe and draw it.
- Plan a day for a student visiting from another country.
- Describe a color without using its name.
- Think of a title for this day.

Some things you can do to promote creativity in yourself include reading, solving puzzles, playing games, traveling, and pursuing hobbies. Even people who are somewhat limited in creative abilities tend to be more creative when doing things they enjoy, things that they do just for the joy of doing them, not for some other reward. The more things you enjoy doing and the more things that spark your interest, the more opportunities you will have to use your creative powers.

RELAXATION · Daydreaming once in a while is good; habitual worry is not. Worry gets in the way of good thinking. It creates mental and emotional pressure, called stress, which is not good for your body or your mind.

It is difficult to pay attention to things when we are under stress. Being upset or fearful uses up energy, leaving less for other mental functions. If you let yourself get really stressed out at school, then you probably aren't doing your best thinking there.

If there's some action you can take to deal with things you worry about, do it. If not, distract yourself; change your thoughts. Don't let the stress continue to build.

Mental relaxation is a way to reduce mental stress and promote creativity. The relaxed person is more likely to operate in a "whole-brained" fashion. Many people find that after taking time to relax their minds, they are refreshed and ready to tackle problems and be creative.

To follow this technique, you need a fairly quiet place, where you will be free from interruption for at least ten to twenty minutes. Choose a comfortable position, sitting or lying down. Close your eyes. Take a couple of deep breaths to relax your body. Think about your body becoming more and more relaxed, your muscles becoming loose and heavy. Try to relax your mind by thinking only about something very simple and quiet, like lying on the beach or listening to a gentle rainfall.

When you're done relaxing, gradually start to flex and stretch different parts of your body. Open your eyes. Give yourself a minute or two to come back to reality.

This technique is a 100-percent-natural, no-chemicals-added, healthy way to relax your body and your mind. It helps to relieve stress that is harmful to your health, and it can leave you better prepared to deal with your problems. It is much better for you than using drugs or alcohol as relaxants. These substances affect the synapses between nerve cells in the brain. They can be very harmful to your ability to think, as well as to your body. They don't solve your problems, and are likely to create new ones.

PROBLEM SOLVING AND DECISION MAKING

One scientist described the difference between human and ape as follows: An ape comes to a river and sees it as a limit—that's as far as it can go in that direction. A person comes to a river and sees it as a problem to solve—how to get across.

Problem solving is where critical and creative thinking come together. The skills you've learned in each of those areas can help you be a better problem solver.

Learning problem-solving methods can help you to do better on tests by allowing you to use knowledge and information you've learned—although problem-solving methods can't help you if you haven't learned the knowledge and information necessary. Problem-solving skills can also help you in life because, as you've probably noticed, everyday life is full of problems.

WORKING PLANS AND GENERAL GUIDES • Problem solving implies that there is something new about the information or situation that you face. There is something that needs to be figured out.

If a situation is familiar, you simply apply known information and skills. This is called an algorithm—a learned, memorized working plan or procedure. For example, you have an algorithm for tying your shoes or making a peanut butter sandwich.

When faced with a new situation or a problem that you don't have a working plan for, you apply a heuristic, or experimental approach for exploration or explanation, such as the trial-and-error method. Everything you have an algorithm for was once a problem requiring heuristic application. For example, if a problem develops between yourself and a friend, do you generally confront the friend about it right away, talk to someone else about it and try to get that person to solve it for you, or pretend that the problem doesn't exist and hope it will go away? Perhaps one of these strategies is a heuristic for you, a general approach you commonly apply to problem-solving situations.

Many situations involve both algorithms and heuristics, applying some knowledge and figuring out something new.

There are two parts to being able to solve problems. The first is to have basic skills and knowledge in the problem areas. Being an expert in a subject can be very helpful in solving problems in that area. People who know a lot about a particular subject tend to have a good understanding of how bits of information fit together. This can help them solve problems quicker and better. Unfortunately, this relates only to problems in their particular area of expertise. A person who knows a lot about plumbing will probably be good at solving plumbing problems. But this knowledge is not likely to be of any help in solving medical problems (or vice versa). And sometimes knowledge can get in the way—an expert may jump too quickly to a solution. Preconceived notions can be like blinders on the problem solver, causing him or her to focus on one possibility while ignoring other possible solutions.

The second part is to have skill in problem-solving strategies. Problem-solving skills are no substitute for learning the subject matter itself. But when these two skill aspects are combined, the odds are good that you will be successful in problem solving.

CREATIVE PROBLEM SOLVING • Beyond the basic steps in problem solving are some strategies that creative problem solvers use. One suggestion to encourage creativity in problem solving is to take an "inside-out" approach. To do this, you start with a clear

Basic Steps in Problem Solving

1. Have a clear understanding of what the problem is. State what needs to be decided, solved, or done. If it's a large problem, break it down into its components. Examine each individually.

2. Gather all pertinent information. Consider all angles of the problem in light of the facts. Keep an open mind; don't jump to conclusions too soon. Consider how this problem is similar to other problems you've solved before. How might things you've tried before work here? Also consider how it is different. Maybe things that *didn't* work before might work here.

3. List as many possible solutions as you can. Don't stop with just a few of the most obvious possibilities. Try to think up new and unusual alternatives.

4. Consider the choices. Think about the possibilities of each alternative. Start to narrow down the list of possible solutions, working toward the best choice. Remain as objective as possible throughout. Try to stick to the facts. Don't let opinions or prejudices block you from possible solutions.

5. Choose the best alternative.

6. Create and implement a plan to put that choice in action. In other words, do what you have decided to do.

7. Evaluate your decision and its effects. Make changes as necessary.

definition of the problem. Then you shift, deliberately, from this left-brain approach to a right-brain approach. This means looking at the problem from a totally different, unusual point of view. For example, imagine that the opposite of the current situation was the problem. How would you deal with that? Taking an inside-out approach allows the right brain to play with the problem.

Another idea is to look at the problem in relation to its environment. This is called looking at the big picture or looking at the space around the problem.

⊁ Reorganization is also a useful problem-solving skill. People using it ask themselves, "How can I change this situation, turn things around, or see them in a different way?" For example, many people tried to figure out how to make an automatic sewing machine, but no one could figure out how to get the eye of the needle all the way through the fabric. They had a preconceived notion of how a needle must look. Elias Howe solved the problem by not letting this preconceived idea get in his way. He put the eye of the needle in the point.

Usually we expect to be able to solve problems in ways that have worked for us before. Sometimes these past experiences help; sometimes they get in the way. The more closely related the present situation is to past experiences, the more likely your past experiences will help. But the past can also be an impediment to problem solving. For example, functional fixedness develops when we see something being used in some way and think that that is the only use. When boxes are full, we see them only as containers. When they are empty we are more easily able to see them as objects with many uses.

Children are less likely to suffer from functional fixedness than adults, perhaps because they have not yet been trained to see things as having just one correct function. When an adult sees a branch on the ground near a tree, he sees a piece of dead

A poster from the 1860s hails the "inventive genius" of Elias Howe. Howe invented the first successful sewing machine by looking at an old problem in a new way.

wood that probably should be gotten rid of because it is no longer "functional." A child seeing the same branch may see a magic wand, a weapon, or a pony to ride.

Here's a problem for you to try. Find six matchsticks or toothpicks of equal length. See if you can arrange them to make four equilateral triangles, the sides of which are each one stick long.

Here's another problem. Copy or trace these nine dots, spaced evenly apart, onto a piece of plain paper. Can you connect all nine dots with four straight lines without lifting your pencil from the paper?

•　　•　　•

•　　•　　•

•　　•　　•

See if you can solve these problems before turning to page 102 to find the solutions.

DECISION MAKING • There are seldom any "perfect" situations in life. Decision making often involves choosing between alternatives when more than one or perhaps none may really be

---

Decisions to be Made

- You've asked your parents if you can go to a party at a friend's house Friday night. How might your parents go about deciding whether or not to let you attend?
- You have to decide whether to take track or band after school. They meet at the same time, so you can't take both. How would you decide which to do?

"good." Decision making is very similar to problem solving. Follow the same basic steps. And recognize that there are pros and cons on almost every issue. If someone is only telling you the pros, he or she is probably not giving you all the information. You need to weigh all the pros and cons and then make the best decision possible. Remember, "The true test of intelligence is not how much we know how to do, but how we behave when we don't know what to do."[4]

INTELLIGENCE

Intelligence is usually equated with mental ability. It is the capacity to acquire and apply knowledge (to learn and to think). More specifically, we usually relate intelligence to problem-solving performance. It also includes the ability to adapt to new situations.

Did you know that you were given a "score" within ten minutes of your birth (assuming you were born in an American hospital)? It's called the Apgar score and reflects how well a baby adapts to the drastic change in scenery it's just experienced.

Our society is obsessed with measuring things—how much, how many, how fast. With the ruler, the stopwatch, and the calculator we measure everything we can. We measure the largest and the smallest things around us, and everything in between. We measure everything we can see and many things we can't.

We even think we've found a way to measure intelligence—something we can't see or touch and even have difficulty defining. We use a measuring tool called an intelligence test, and we turn the result of that test into a number: the intelligence quotient, or IQ.

INTELLIGENCE AND IQ • An IQ of 100 is average. It means that 50 percent of the people of the same age score at that level or better, and 50 percent score at that level or lower.

Intelligence is more than something you are either born with or not. Intelligence is related to environment. Scientists disagree about exactly how much our intelligence level is dictated by our genes, and how much can be related to environment. It is generally agreed, however, that environment and genes both play a part in the development of IQ. A child who grows up in an environment that encourages good study habits, persistence, and the acquisition of knowledge is more likely to do well on intelligence tests than a child who grows up in an environment without this encouragement. And a change in that environment is likely to yield a change in intelligence as measured by IQ tests.

There are cases where children who scored extremely low on intelligence tests have had their IQ scores raised significantly and have gone on to be successful in various careers. While these cases are extreme, they do show that (at least in some cases) intelligence can be raised.

Critics of IQ tests say that the decision to label someone "intelligent" depends on what questions we ask and whom we compare a respondent with. They say that the dominant culture decides what is important enough to be included on IQ tests. Often the tests don't value the things that minorities learn, and those things are not included. If they were, minorities would score higher, and members of the dominant culture would score lower.

IQ tests are sometimes used to predict how well children will do in school. To do well on an intelligence test, a child needs to be able to recall and recognize words, numbers, and ideas. These are skills that are important in school. So if you are good at these things you will be good at IQ tests and at school. But there are many other factors to take into consideration. Motivation and personality are important factors, as are environment, opportunity, and outside encouragement. Highly mo-

tivated students with average IQ scores are likely to have better grades in school than students who score higher but find school boring or are simply lazy.

And there is more to success in life than success in school. There are many skills that take brainpower that aren't measured by IQ tests, and that people with high IQ may or may not be good at. Such skills include the ability to be creative—to invent new ways of looking at words, numbers, and ideas. Physical skills are not measured either—running, dancing, and the ability to manipulate things with your hands. It takes brainpower to be athletic.

Other skills not measured by IQ include a sense of humor, the ability to think and act independently, an appreciation of beauty, and the ability to compromise and change, to be flexible. Many careers require these skills as much as if not more than abilities that can be measured by IQ tests. This is why IQ tests are not good at predicting how successful people will be in life.

Most IQ tests and other tests given in schools require that you think convergently—they have one right answer. But many real-life situations require divergent thinking—there are many possible right answers. You have to choose the best option from many alternatives. While schools tend to reward one-right-answer convergent thinking, life often rewards new-and-creative-solution divergent thinking.

MULTIPLE INTELLIGENCES • If intelligence is described as brainpower, there must be many kinds of intelligence, because there are many different kinds of activities that require brainpower.

What are the types of abilities included in intelligence? How many are there? Is each as important as the others? Some say there are two, some say there are more than a hundred.

From the time they are born, American children are presented with dozens of tests that measure mental abilities.

Researcher Howard Gardner identified seven types of intelligence: linguistic, musical, logical-mathematical, spatial, bodily-kinesthetic, intrapersonal, and interpersonal.

Linguistic intelligence involves the mastery of language. It is expressed in our ability to grasp the variations in meanings of words. The vast majority of human beings exhibit a fairly good amount of linguistic intelligence—most people can communicate with words. We use language to help us think, to organize information in our minds. We also use language to explain ourselves to others, to convince others to think or do as we want, and to entertain ourselves and others. Linguistic intelligence is particularly important for all writers, and especially for poets.

Musical intelligence is the ability to understand and manipulate melody and rhythm to create music. Melody and rhythm are to musical intelligence what words are to linguistic. This intelligence is being used when we sing, play an instrument, or compose music.

Logical-mathematical intelligence is also sometimes called scientific intelligence. This intelligence deals with our need to order, organize, and assess the world of objects. With logical-mathematical intelligence an individual can perform actions with and upon objects and can move from actions to statements about relations between objects. A baby stacking blocks, knocking them down, and then stacking them the same way again is beginning to develop this intelligence.

With spatial intelligence we are able to accurately perceive the visual world, as well as to transform and re-create the objects that we see. This includes the ability to create mental pictures. This intelligence is very useful in conjunction with other intelligences. For example, Albert Einstein, very skilled in mathematical intellect, was also gifted with spatial intelligence. Thus he could visualize himself riding on a beam of light, and this imagery helped him to solve difficult mathematical problems. Artists of all kinds tend to be able to use spatial intelligence well.

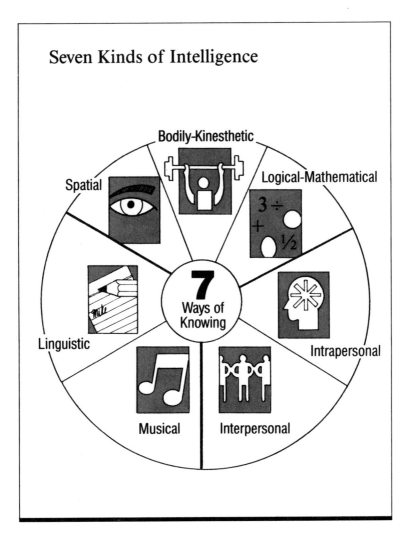

Seven Kinds of Intelligence

Bodily-Kinesthetic

Spatial

Logical-Mathematical

$3 \div$

$+$

$\frac{1}{2}$

7 Ways of Knowing

Intrapersonal

Linguistic

Musical

Interpersonal

Bodily-kinesthetic intelligence allows us to use and to move our bodies in particularly purposeful ways. This includes the athlete's and the dancer's ability to move the entire body or to direct particular muscles, as well as the musician's and the sculptor's talent at manipulating objects with the hands. Sometimes we forget that such physical activity requires a great deal of mental activity as well.

Intrapersonal intelligence is the understanding and appreciation of the self. It helps us understand what gives us pleasure and what causes us pain. When you are reflective, quietly thinking about yourself and your personal thought processes, you are using this intelligence. We begin to develop this ability at an early age and continue throughout our lives.

Interpersonal intelligence also deals with the self, but it is the relationship between the self and others that is key here. It is what helps the child know when to press mom or dad for permission to do something and when to back off. It is what you use when you act one way in front of your friends and another way in front of your grandparents. Anyone who deals with other people—from politicians to salespersons to teachers—can benefit from developing interpersonal intelligence.

Gardner believes that all people possess all seven intelligences, although each of us uses them to different degrees in different situations. A combination of genetic talent and the experiences that our environment exposes us to shapes each of us as a unique blend of these intelligences. Many researchers now agree that intelligence can be described as a range of abilities. A person who is strong in most of these abilities is considered more intelligent than a person who is weak in most of them.

INTELLIGENCE AND HEALTH • Some people worry that the average intelligence level of the general population may be slipping. They cite such causes as poor nutrition (which means not only not enough food, but food high in sugar and chemical additives) and excessive TV watching.

There are things that we can do to promote the development of intelligence throughout our lives. Show respect for the body that houses your brain. Feed it right. Proper nutrition is vitally important for optimal brain development. At least thirty-seven of the forty-four nutrients required by the human body are needed for brain development. Avoid polluting your body and brain with unhealthy substances.

Respect your internal body rhythms. Exercise and play, relaxation and sleep—all are needed.

Mental stimulation affects intelligence. Researchers found that the brains of rats that had been exposed to a highly stimulating environment, with lots to see and do, were more highly developed. That has led some people to suggest that you should limit the amount of TV you watch. Watching TV is a passive activity that generally stimulates only the lower-level centers of the brain. It robs you of time that would be better spent on brain-stimulating activities.

These and other factors help us to reach our fullest intelligence potential.

CONCLUSION: PUTTING YOUR MIND TO WORK

We've seen that perception is our ability to absorb. Learning is our ability to retain, and memory is our storehouse of knowledge retained. Thinking is our ability to manipulate material in our minds.

All these skills are interconnected. In this book we've looked at them separately. But keep in mind that whole-brain—and in fact whole-body—learning is best. Whole-brain learning means using both left and right hemispheres, a variety of learning styles and modalities, and as many of our different intelligence areas as possible. Whole-body learning means acknowledging that the brain is part of the body and that each affects the other.

We live in a world where things are constantly changing. No society before ours has had to face the problem of coping with so much change so rapidly. And the world is going to keep on changing. You can either be one of the movers and shapers, causing positive changes to happen, or you can bury your head, moan and complain, and be left behind to let others make the changes that will affect you. If you'd rather be one of the people in charge, even if that means just being in charge of your own life, you will have to be good at using as much of your brain as possible.

There are many reasons to work at increasing your brainpower. Author Win Wenger lists a few: "Greater success obtainable in career, improved schoolwork, longer healthier life, greater ease in solving your present problems."5 It is in your best interest to increase your brainpower.

Today it is more critical than ever for people to know how to think and how to learn. There's just no way that teachers can give you all the information you will need. You have to know where to go to find it for yourself. You have to know how to evaluate the information that you find. You have to know how to process information to come up with new and creative solutions to problems that never existed before.

People have a wide range of talents and abilities. As we grow, we learn to learn, and we learn to think. As we continue to grow, we continue to perfect these skills. It is up to you to find the areas you are most interested in and most talented at and pursue them. It is also up to you to strengthen the areas that you are not as naturally gifted at.

The assumptions you make about your abilities will make a difference in your level of success. Believing that you are capable increases the likelihood that you will be.

Authors Kurt Hanks and Jay Parry draw our attention to the fact that most of us use only about 10 percent of our total brainpower. They add, "Part of the problem is our laziness. It's easy to let someone else do our creative thinking for us. At their jobs, a lot of people do only what they're told. At home we let television baby-sit us, stealing from us opportunities to think, imagine, dream, invent, create."6

Peter Kline puts it this way: "Somewhere inside of you is your own sort of genius—waiting and wondering when you'll care enough to call it forth."7

The mind is at work no matter what you are doing. The person at work in a garden or behind a desk or under a car or up on a telephone pole is using his or her mind. But a person who makes the most of mind power, who takes care of brain and body, is likely to be healthier, happier, and more successful. That's what putting your mind to work for you is all about.

Solutions

The six sticks:

The problem can
be solved only with
a three-dimensional
approach. Form

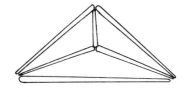

one triangle by placing three sticks flat on the table.
Stand the remaining three upright in the corners so that
they join at the top in a three-sided pyramid.

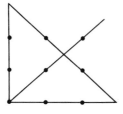

The nine dots:

The directions said nothing about not
going beyond the dots. That is a limit
you may have placed on yourself.

SOURCE NOTES

1. Robert Fulghum, *All I Really Need to Know I Learned in Kindergarten* (New York: Ballantine Books, 1986).

2. In particular David Kolb, author of *Experiential Learning* (Englewood Cliffs, NJ: Prentice-Hall, 1984), and Bernice McCarthy, author of *The 4MAT System* (Barrington, IL: EXCEL Inc., 1987).

3. Morton Hunt, *The Universe Within* (New York: Simon and Schuster, 1982), p. 22.

4. John Holt, quoted in Gilbert Stevenson, *Igniting Creative Potential* (Salt Lake City: Project Implode, 1971).

5. Win Wenger, *How to Increase Your Intelligence* (Indianapolis: Bobbs-Merrill, 1975), p. 26.

6. Kurt Hanks and Jay Parry, *Wake Up Your Creative Genius* (Los Altos, CA: William Kaufmann, 1983), p. 25.

7. Peter Kline, *The Everyday Genius* (Arlington, VA: Great Ocean Publishers, 1988), p. 186.

RECOMMENDED READING AND BIBLIOGRAPHY

The following books are recommended for further reading.

On the brain and its functions:

Bailey, Ronald H. *The Role of the Brain*. Alexandria, VA: Time-Life Books, 1975.

Berger, Melvin. *Exploring the Mind and Brain*. New York: Thomas Y. Crowell, 1983.

Facklam, Margery and Howard. *The Brain: Magnificent Mind Machine*. New York: Harcourt Brace Jovanovich, 1982.

Haines, Gail Kay. *Brain Power: Understanding Human Intelligence*. New York: Franklin Watts, 1979.

Kettelkamp, Larry. *The Human Brain*. Hillside, NJ: Enslow, 1986.

Silverstein, Alvin and Virginia. *World of the Brain*. New York: William Morrow, 1986.

On perception:

Messengers to the Brain: Our Fantastic Five Senses. Washington, DC: National Geographic Society, 1984.

O'Neill, Catherine. *You Won't Believe Your Eyes*. Washington, DC: National Geographic Society, 1987.

On learning:

Edson, Lee. *How We Learn.* Alexandria, VA: Time-Life Books, 1975.

Ohme, Herman. *Learn How to Learn.* Los Angeles: California Education Plan, 1986.

Tchudi, Stephen. *The Young Learner's Handbook.* New York: Charles Scribner's Sons, 1987.

Wirths, Claudine, and Mary Bowman-Kruhm. *I Hate School: How to Hang In and When to Drop Out.* New York: Thomas Y. Crowell, 1987.

On memory:

Gallant, Roy A. *Memory.* New York: Four Winds Press, 1980.

Gilbert, Sara. *How to Take Tests.* New York: William Morrow, 1983.

Halacy, Don. *How to Improve Your Memory.* New York: Franklin Watts, 1977.

Meltzer, Milton. *The Landscape of Memory.* New York: Viking Kestrel, 1987.

**On thinking,
critical thinking, and
problem solving:**

Burns, Marilyn. *The Book of Think.* Boston: Little, Brown, 1976.

Cohen, Daniel. *Re-Thinking.* New York: Evans, 1982.

Klein, David and Marymae Klein. *How Do You Know It's True?* New York: Charles Scribner's Sons, 1984.

Loeb, Robert H., Jr. *The Sins of Bias.* New York: M. Evans, 1970.

On creativity:

Mott, Jacolyn A. *Creativity and Imagination.* Mankato, MN: Creative Education, 1973.

Wetherall, Charles A. *The Gifted Kids' Guide to Creative Thinking.* Wetherall, 1984.

On intelligence:

Cohen, Daniel. *Intelligence: What Is It?* New York: M. Evans, 1974.

Ehrenberg, Miriam, and Otto Ehrenberg. *Optimum Brain Power: A Total Program for Increasing Your Intelligence.* New York: Dodd, Mead, 1985.

Gilbert, Sara. *Using Your Head: The Many Ways to Be School Smart.* New York: Macmillan, 1984.

James, Elizabeth, and Carol Barkin. *How to Be School Smart.* New York: Lothrop, Lee and Shepard, 1988.

The following books were also helpful in writing this book.

Albrecht, Karl. *Brain Power. Learn to Improve Your Thinking Skills.* New York: Prentice Hall Press, 1980.

Arieti, Silvana. *Creativity —The Magic Synthesis.* New York: Basic Books, 1976.

Beadle, Muriel. *A Child's Mind.* New York: Doubleday, 1970.

Borass, Julius. *Teaching to Think.* New York: Macmillan, 1922.

Bower, T.G.R. *The Perceptual World of the Child.* Cambridge, MA: Harvard University Press, 1977.

Brookfield, Stephen. *Developing Critical Thinkers.* San Francisco, CA: Jossey-Bass, 1987.

Buzan, Tony. *Use Both Sides of Your Brain.* New York: Penguin Group, 1989.

Cantor, Nathaniel. *The Dynamics of Learning.* New York: Henry Stewart, 1946.

Cohen, Laura. *Decision Making.* Compton, CA: Educational Insights, 1985.

Conners, C. Keith. *Feeding the Brain.* New York: Plenum Press, 1989.

Edwards, Betty. *Drawing on the Artist Within.* New York: Simon and Schuster, 1986.

Ehrlich, Paul R., and S. Shirley Feldman. *The Race Book: Skin Color, Prejudice, and Intelligence.* New York: New York Times Book Co., 1977.

Fincher, Jack. *Human Intelligence.* New York: G. P. Putnam's Sons, 1976.

Gardner, Howard. *Frames of Mind.* New York: Basic Books, 1983.

_____. *The Unschooled Mind. How Children Think and How Schools Should Teach.* New York: Basic Books, 1991.

Gazzaniga, Michael. *Mind Matters.* Boston: Houghton Mifflin, 1988.

Guild, Pat Burke, and Stephen Garger. *Marching to Different Drummers.* Alexandria, VA: Association for Supervision and Curriculum Development, 1985.

Hanks, Kurt, and Jay A. Parry. *Wake Up Your Creative Genius.* Los Altos, CA: William Kaufmann, 1983.

Healy, Jane M. *Endangered Minds. Why Our Children Don't Think.* New York: Simon and Schuster, 1990.

Hunt, Morton. *The Universe Within.* New York: Simon and Schuster, 1982.

Kline, Peter. *The Everyday Genius.* Arlington, VA: Great Ocean Publishers, 1988.

Kolb, David A. *Experiential Learning.* Englewood Cliffs, NJ: Prentice-Hall, 1984.

Link, Frances R. *Essays on the Intellect.* Alexandria, VA: Association for Supervision and Curriculum Development, 1985.

Mattson, Carol. *Misfits in School.* Saratoga, CA: R & E Publishers, 1985.

May, Rollo. *The Courage to Create.* New York: W. W. Norton and Co., 1975.

Mayer, Richard. *Thinking, Problem Solving, Cognition.* New York: W. H. Freeman and Co., 1983.

McCarthy, Bernice. *The 4MAT System.* Barrington, IL: EXCEL Inc., 1987.

McConnell, James V. *Understanding Human Behavior.* New York: Holt, Rinehart, Winston, 1980.

Ornstein, Robert, and Richard Thompson. *The Amazing Brain.* Boston: Houghton Mifflin, 1984.

Osborn, Alex. *Applied Imagination.* New York: Charles Scribner's Sons, 1963.

Papert, Seymour. *Mindstorms: Children, Computers and Powerful Ideas.* New York: Basic Books, 1980.

Postman, Neil, and Charles Weingartner. *Teaching as a Subversive Activity.* New York: Delacorte Press, 1969.

Prince, Francine, and Harold Prince. *Feed Your Kids Bright.* New York: Simon and Schuster, 1987.

Restak, Richard. *The Brain.* New York: Bantam Books, 1984.

————. *The Mind.* New York: Bantam Books, 1988.

Russell, Peter. *The Brain Book.* New York: Hawthorn Books, 1979.

Smith, Robert M. *Learning How to Learn.* Chicago: Follett, 1982.

Spencer Pulaski, Mary Ann. *Understanding Piaget.* New York: Harper and Row, 1971.

Springer, Sally P., and Georg Deutsch. *Left Brain, Right Brain.* San Francisco: W. H. Freeman and Co., 1981.

Sternberg, Robert J. *How Can We Teach Intelligence?* Research for Better Schools, 1983.

Stevenson, Gilbert M. *Igniting Creative Potential.* Salt Lake City: Project Implode, 1971.

Van Gundy, Arthur B. *Training Your Creative Mind.* Englewood Cliffs, NJ: Prentice-Hall, 1982.

Wenger, Win. *How to Increase Your Intelligence.* Indianapolis: Bobbs-Merrill Co., 1975.

Wilson, John Rowan. *The Mind.* New York: Time-Life Books, 1969.

Wonder, Jacquelyn. *Whole Brain Thinking.* New York: William Morrow, 1984.

Youngs, Dr. Bettie B. *Stress in Children.* New York: Arbor House, 1985.

INDEX

Musical intelligence, 96

Names, 56
Neurochemistry, 15
Neurons, 19–20, 47
Neurotransmitters, 19–20
Note-taking, 52
Nutrition, 21–22, 98

Occipital lobe, 17
Output, 40, 41

Parietal lobe, 17, 18
Parry, Jan, 101
Pavlov, Ivan, 32
Perception, 12, 23–28, 100
Perseverance, 43
Piaget, Jean, 33, *34*, 35
Positron-emission tomography
   (PET), 13, *16*
Practice, 43
Prejudice, 59
Print-oriented learning, 39, 40
Problem solving, 85–88, 90
Proteins, 21

Rationalization, 61
Reading, 40, 41
Recall, 47
Recognition, 46
Redintegration, 47
Relaxation, 83–84
Renoir, Pierre Auguste, 75
Reorganization, 88
Residual memory, 47
Review, 53–54
Rhythm and rhyme, 51

Right hemisphere of brain, 17–
   19, 62–64, 78, 79, 87, 88,
   100

Saturation, 77–79
Scientific intelligence, 96
Sensations, 23
Senses, 12, 25, 37
Short-term memory, 47–49, 53
Socrates, 55, 57
Spatial intelligence, 96
Spatial relationships, 63
Spinal cord, 15
Stereotypes, 59, 75
Stress, 83–84
Styles of learning, 37–40
Synapses, 19, 84
Synectics, 82
Synthesis, 40

Television watching, 29, 98, 99
Temporal lobe, 17, 18
Tests, 54
Thalamus, 17
Thinking, 12, 55–64, 100
   creative, 74–84
   critical, 65–73
Time management, 44
Toscanini, Arturo, 50

Van Gogh, Vincent, 75
Vision, 26–27
Visual learning, 39
Vitamins, 21–22

Wenger, Win, 101
Working conditions, 42
Worry, 83–84

ABOUT THE AUTHOR

Eileen Lucas's interest in the workings of the mind was sparked by a high-school seminar on critical and creative thinking. She continued to be intrigued by the subject in college and as she developed her career as a nonfiction writer. This book is the result of that lifelong interest. Her previous books for young readers have covered such topics as conflict resolution, acid rain, and the water supply. She is also the author of several biographies, among them *Jane Goodall: Friend of the Chimps* from The Millbrook Press. She lives in Fontana, Wisconsin, with her husband and two sons.